GOING GREEN

A Kid's Handbook
to Saving the Planet

John Elkington, Julia Hailes
Douglas Hill, and Joel Makower

Illustrated by Tony Ross

A Tilden Press Book

VIKING

VIKING
Published by the Penguin Group
Viking Penguin, a division of Penguin Books USA Inc.,
375 Hudson Street, New York, New York 10014, U.S.A.
Penguin Books Ltd, 27 Wrights Lane, London W8 5TZ, England
Penguin Books Australia Ltd, Ringwood, Victoria, Australia
Penguin Books Canada Ltd, 2801 John Street, Markham, Ontario, Canada L3R 1B4
Penguin Books (N.Z.) Ltd, 182–190 Wairau Road, Auckland 10, New Zealand

Penguin Books Ltd, Registered Offices: Harmondsworth, Middlesex, England

First published in Great Britain as *The Young Green Consumer Guide* by Victor Gollancz Ltd, 1990
First American edition published 1990
1   3   5   7   9   10   8   6   4   2
Text copyright © John Elkington, Julia Hailes, Douglas Hill,
and Viking Penguin, a division of Penguin Books USA, Inc., 1990
Illustrations copyright © Tony Ross, 1990
All rights reserved

LIBRARY OF CONGRESS CATALOGING-IN-PUBLICATION DATA
Going green : a kid's handbook to save the planet / by John
Elkington . . . [et al.] ; illustrated by Tony Ross.   p.   cm.
Summary: A guide to saving the environment, including explanations
of ecological issues and projects.
ISBN 0-670-83611-7
1. Environmental protection—Citizen participation—Juvenile
literature.   [1. Environmental protection.]   I. Elkington, John.
II. Ross, Tony, ill.
TD171.7.G64   1990   363.7′0525—dc20   90-12682

Printed in the United States of America
by R.R. Donnelley & Sons Company, Willard, Ohio
Optima

Contents

All over the world, kids just like you are helping to save the Earth. Really. They may not feel powerful or important, but they are.

"How can this be?" you may be asking. "I'm just me, and even with all of my friends and neighbors and classmates it's not a very large group. After all, the world has billions of people!"

Well, a lot of those people are kids. And more and more kids are becoming aware of the environment. Many of them are doing something about it. You can be sure that when millions of kids all start doing the same thing, the entire world will sit up and take notice.

So, *you* have the power to change the world!

You've probably heard some things about the environment on the news or from your teachers or parents. Maybe you've heard about pollution, or the ozone layer, or the rainforests, or the greenhouse effect. You probably are confused about what some of these things mean. Don't worry—most grown-ups are confused, too.

Some of these problems sound so big and far away! The ozone layer is thousands of miles in the sky. The rainforests are mostly on other continents. How can you possibly do anything about these problems?

The fact is, when kids talk, grown-ups listen. And when kids do things, grown-ups pay attention. You don't have to be famous or rich or important to get grownups to listen. You just have to ask.

So, what are *you* going to do?

ARE YOU A GREEN CONSUMER?

One of the ways you can do something is to become a "Green Consumer." What exactly is a Green Consumer? It is someone who recognizes that every time you shop, you are casting a vote "for" or "against" the environment. It doesn't matter what you are shopping for—candy, records, clothes, food, or even cars. Everything you buy is another vote. If everyone votes "for" as much as possible, we can make a big difference in protecting the Earth.

So, you want to make decisions that vote "for" the environment as much as possible!

You'd be surprised to learn just how much power you have as a Green Consumer. By casting votes "for" things that don't harm the environment, you will be forcing companies that make harmful products to make changes. If they don't change, they could go out of business.

Shopping is just one part of being a Green Consumer. It also has to do with the things you do every day, from how you get to school to what you throw away. You probably don't realize it, but you cast "votes" dozens of times a day! As you understand this better, you may want to do some things differently.

One of the best things you can do is to talk to grown-ups about the environment. Your parents, teachers, store owners, government officials, and other adults care a lot about what you think. They will listen to you!

It is also important that you ask a lot of questions. This book is full of questions to ask and other things to find out. Make sure you get the answers you are looking for. If you don't, keep asking! Many people won't know the answers to some of your questions. But maybe they *should* know. They may not have thought of the question before. By asking, you may get them thinking.

You can change things just by asking!

So, remember: You have a lot of power. You can use that power to help solve some of the most important problems in the world. All you have to do is understand what's going on and ask some good questions.

You can do it!

What's Going On?

Just like you, the planet Earth needs to stay in good health in order to function at its best. Without good health, the Earth wouldn't be able to do those things we need most: grow plants and animals, give us clean air and water, provide beautiful places for us to visit, and all the other things we take for granted each day.

What exactly is wrong with the Earth? The first step in "going green" is to understand the environmental problems our planet faces. Let's take a brief look around. . . .

——The Greenhouse Effect——

Have you ever sat in front of a sunny window on a cold, cold day? As the sun came in through the window, you baked in its heat, even though outside it was quite chilly, maybe even below freezing. Why was it so warm?

Your toasty window does two things. It lets the sun shine in and prevents much of the heat from escaping outside. So, your window is a heat trap. Imagine how hot it would get on a sunny day if you lived in a house made entirely of windows!

You've just learned how the Greenhouse Effect works.

The Earth is surrounded by windows, too. We call these windows the **atmosphere**, a layer of air many miles up in the sky. As the sun shines on the Earth, the atmosphere lets the heat reach the ground, then prevents some of it from escaping back into space.

That's all fine. In fact, we need the atmosphere. Without it, the Earth would be as cold and lifeless as the surface of the moon. The problem is that our atmosphere is changing. Some of our favorite activities create gases that pollute the atmosphere. As those gases build up, the atmosphere keeps in too much heat.

8

WHAT ARE GREENHOUSE GASES?

You can't see or feel the gases as they drift up into the atmosphere, but they are a serious problem. What exactly are these gases?

☛The most important is **carbon dioxide**, also known as CO_2. All humans and animals produce CO_2 every time we exhale, but there's nothing we can do about that. The main source of CO_2 pollution is the burning of fossil fuels—coal, oil, and gasoline—and wood.

☛Another greenhouse gas is **nitrogen oxide**, which is given off by cars as we drive them and by coal-burning power plants as they generate electricity.

☛Still another is **methane**, which is created by rotting plants and by household garbage as it deteriorates in landfills. (Humans and other animals also create methane—every time we pass gas.)

☛The final gases are **chlorofluorocarbons** or CFCs. We'll discuss those more on page 11.

We've been creating all of these gases for a long time. But now we're producing too much of them and they are making the Earth a little hotter. So far, the change is so small that it's hardly noticeable. But it still is happening.

Some people, especially those living in the north, think it might be nice to have a warmer climate. But things aren't that simple. Here's what could happen if average temperatures on Earth increased just a few degrees:

☛Some of the ice around the North Pole and the South Pole would melt.

☛That melted ice would cause the sea levels to rise.

☛People living near sea level could be flooded.

☛Some places would become too hot to live in.

☛Many farmers' crops would no longer grow.

Some scientists now think that the average temperatures on Earth could rise by between 3 and 10 degrees Fahrenheit by the middle of the next century. If that happened, water levels could flood much of New York

City. In Washington, D.C., water would flood the Lincoln Memorial and nearly reach the Capitol steps!

That's just the beginning. As things got even warmer, hundreds of different living creatures could die and become extinct, while many kinds of pests (such as rats and mosquitoes) could multiply in the warmer climate.

THE EARTH'S NATURAL REMEDIES

Just as some of the greenhouse gases are produced naturally, some of the gases are also soaked up naturally. Sea water soaks up carbon dioxide, and so do the tiny organisms in the sea called plankton. But because plankton soaks up more CO_2 in colder water, as the Greenhouse Effect warms the oceans, the plankton will absorb less carbon dioxide.

Plants on land also soak up CO_2, especially the trees in the mighty rainforests of the world. But because trees in the rainforests are being cut down and burned, there are fewer trees to soak up the greenhouses gases. What's worse, the burning of trees actually produces even more CO_2, contributing to the greenhouse problem. In fact, rainforest burning is one of the greatest contributors to the Greenhouse Effect (see page 18 for more on this).

Many scientists believe that the Greenhouse Effect has already started to affect us. They point to unusual changes in the weather—mild winters and very hot summers in some parts of the United States, for example. But, they say, it's not too late to ease the problem.

WHAT CAN YOU DO?

One big way to help is to cut down on the use of energy. Every time you turn on the lights, open the refrigerator, turn on the heat, or take a ride in the car, you are using energy—electricity, gasoline, and natural gas, for example. The power plants that generate the electricity and the automobile engines that burn gasoline all create vast amounts of CO_2.

This doesn't mean that you'll have to live in a cold, dark house, or that you won't be able to drive anywhere. As you'll see later on in this book, it simply means using energy resources carefully.

—Holes in the Ozone Layer—

Ozone is an invisible gas, a form of oxygen. A thin layer of ozone exists between 12 and 30 miles (20 to 50 kilometers) above the Earth and forms a protective shield that is vital to our survival. Without it, the sun would burn us, and few things would grow.

The ozone layer shields us from one particular kind of sunlight: ultraviolet (UV) light. Some UV light is important—it helps plants to grow, for example. UV light also gives people a suntan. But if much more UV light were allowed to filter through the ozone layer, it would cause some big problems. Millions of people could get eye and skin diseases, farmers' crops could become damaged, and fish could run out of food.

THE DANGERS OF CHLOROFLUOROCARBONS

What is destroying the ozone layer? One of the biggest culprits is a family of chemicals called chlorofluorocarbons (pronounced *KLOR–o-floor-o-CAR-bons*), or CFCs. These are used in manufacturing hundreds of different products, including many that you and your parents buy regularly. Some kinds of plastics and foam packaging materials are made with CFCs. They are also used to keep refrigerators and air conditioners cool.

Why are CFCs so bad? When they are released into the atmosphere and interact with sunlight, CFCs release chlorine atoms. As they rise into the atmosphere, these chlorine atoms attack and destroy parts of the ozone layer. A single chlorine atom can destroy thousands of ozone molecules. Think of it like a Pac Man video game, where each of the Pac Men go around gobbling things up. That's what CFCs do to the ozone layer.

In 1985, scientists noticed that the ozone layer was not just thinning, but that there was actually a big hole in it over Antarctica. A *very* big hole. By 1987 it had stretched to cover an area the size of the United States. In 1988, scientists found another hole, this time over the Arctic. The holes constantly change shape and size, depending on the time of year.

In 1990, many countries agreed to cut the use of CFCs substantially by the year 2000. Environmentalists hope that we can make a complete switch from CFCs even sooner. Several companies around the world are researching substances that can replace CFCs in air conditioners, refrigerators, plastics, and in many manufacturing processes.

The fact is, even if we were to stop using CFCs today, the existing chemicals would ensure the continued destruction of the ozone layer for at least a century! So, the sooner we stop, the less destruction of the ozone layer we will cause in the future.

WHAT CAN YOU DO?

The main thing you can do is avoid using products that contain CFCs. This isn't always easy to do because CFCs are used in thousands of products, including egg cartons, bicycle seats, toy stuffing, furniture cushions, yogurt machines, cameras, computers, TV sets, radios, and jewelry. But some products, such as plastic foam packaging, are easier to avoid. (Although fast-food containers usually do not contain CFCs, they contribute to the growing pile of trash. So, you should avoid them whenever possible.)

— *Air Pollution and Acid Rain* —

You may have some firsthand experience with air pollution, because almost every city—and even parts of the country—have polluted air. In fact, some of the most beautiful parts of the United States have polluted air, including the Grand Canyon in Arizona, the Everglades in Florida, and Yosemite National Park in California.

How did the air get this bad? Electricity production—the pollution generated by power plants—has contrib-

uted a lot to poor air quality. Cars are another big problem. While the cars made today pollute far less than cars made a few years ago, there are many more cars on the road today, and the typical car drives more miles each year than ever before. As a result, air pollution from cars hasn't decreased much.

In some areas, such as Los Angeles, air pollution has become so bad that the government has been forced to restrict many everyday activities, including driving a car, having a barbecue, even mowing the lawn with a power mower. All of these activities contribute to air pollution.

What's wrong with air pollution? When the air gets too dirty, it can be uncomfortable to breathe, and with every breath you may be inhaling substances that can make you sick. But even when the air is only a little polluted, the effects can still cause many illnesses, particularly among very young children and older adults like your grandparents.

That's not all. Air pollution also hurts plants and animals. It can poison trees and crops, and may even kill entire forests.

WHEN THE RAIN BECOMES POISON

We used to count on a good rainfall to cleanse the air of pollutants. Now, in some parts of the United States, even the rain is polluted. We call it "acid rain," even though the problem also pollutes the snow, sleet, hail, and even fog!

What turns the rain into poison? The problem comes primarily from the burning of fossil fuels, including gasoline burned in automobile engines and oil used for cooking and heating. The biggest source is the burning of coal—especially certain kinds of coal that contain high levels of sulfur—in electric-generating plants.

All of these sources release either sulfur dioxide or nitrogen oxides. Once in the air, these two substances mix with other chemicals and water to form sulfuric acid. When these chemicals mix with moisture, they fall to Earth, where they can cause a great deal of harm.

What happens to acid rain when it reaches the ground? For one thing, it poisons fish and other things that live in rivers, lakes, and streams. It also kills trees. Buildings and monuments can also be affected. Some of the oldest and most treasured buildings in the world have been found to have damage caused by acid rain.

Acid rain also affects people. Some scientists see it as a threat to human health, causing lung disease and other serious problems. Babies, senior citizens, and people who have respiratory diseases such as asthma and bronchitis are among those most seriously affected by acid rain.

A LITTLE EXPERIMENT

You can see the effects of acid rain for yourself. You'll need two houseplants, ideally the same kind. (Don't do this without permission from whomever is in charge of the plants.)

Place the plants side by side so they receive the same amount of sunlight. Then, whenever the plants need watering, give them the same amount, but add a few teaspoons of lemon juice or vinegar to one's water supply.

Watch the plants grow over the next two weeks. Chances are, the one which received the water and lemon juice or vinegar—both of which are highly acidic—isn't growing as well as the other plant. In fact, it will eventually die.

That's how acid affects plants. It also affects trees, insects, fish, animals, and humans.

WHAT CAN YOU DO?

The most important thing you can do is to conserve energy wisely. The less we use, the less we must generate through polluting power plants. As you'll see, there are many things you can do to reduce your energy use—without limiting the activities you've always done.

Later on in this book, we'll offer suggestions on products that use less energy, and we'll describe many things you can do to reduce your energy use.

When you turn on the tap, you expect the water to be clean and drinkable. And you always expect that there will be enough there when you need it.

But finding enough fresh water is getting harder. For one thing, there are more people on the planet, and that requires more water for washing, growing food, and sustaining life. All those people create a lot of waste, some of which ends up polluting rivers, lakes, and streams. And companies that dump hazardous substances into the water make the problem even worse.

The water in your home is probably pumped from rivers and reservoirs. The more water you use, the more likely it is that some beautiful valley will be flooded as a reservoir, or that some river will begin to run dry, killing the wildlife in and around it. And the more dirty water you send down the drain, the more difficult it is for the sewage system to cope. Accidental overflows of sewage can seriously pollute land and water.

WHAT POLLUTES THE WATER?

There are many, many sources of water pollution, some of which may surprise you. We usually think of huge pipes dumping industrial waste into rivers, but only about 10 percent of water pollution comes from industrial dumping.

To fully understand what pollutes water, it is first important to understand where your drinking water comes from. Nearly half of all Americans and three-fourths of those who live in cities get their water from underground sources. Underground water picks up whatever it passes through. Rainwater and melted snow—

HOW MUCH DO YOU USE?

It is difficult to imagine how much water is used in your home every day. Here is a rough guide:

1 flush of the toilet	3.5-7 gallons
1 bath	25-30 gallons
1 10-minute shower	50-70 gallons
1 washing machine load	25-40 gallons
1 dishwasher load	9.5-12 gallons

Try to figure out approximately how many gallons of water you use in your home. If your home is typical, each member of your household uses about 80 gallons of water a day. That's a lot of water, and the less we use, the better it will be for the environment.

running off parking lots, rooftops, streets, and farms—carry with them deadly substances. During a storm, the pollutants are washed into rivers and streams. And once they get into the water cycle, they never seem to leave.

One big source of pollution is farmers. Farming uses about two-thirds of all water in the United States. Every year, millions of pounds of pesticides and fertilizers run off of farmland and contaminate the water supply.

WHAT CAN YOU DO?

There are two things you can do: don't waste water and don't be a polluter. Later on in this book, we'll tell you about devices you and your parents can install at home to save water. You'll also learn some of the things your family does and buys that may pollute the water. And we'll offer some tips on reporting water polluters in your community.

-Saving the Plants and Animals-

Because humans are the smartest creatures on Earth, we do pretty much what we want. If we decide to kill other animals for their fur and skin, there is little that can stop us. If we want to cut down a forest to create a farm or a city, the decision is pretty much up to us.

We are beginning to discover that what we want to do isn't necessarily good for the Earth—and its citizens. For example:

☛We cut down millions of acres of rainforests each year, mostly to create farmland for raising beef. Some of the wood is turned into lumber, but most is simply burned. Because trees are natural storehouses of carbon dioxide, cutting down and burning trees releases CO_2 into the atmosphere, which contributes to global warming.

☛Cutting down the rainforests destroys thousands of plants, animals, and insects that can help humans. Scientists estimate that between 5 million and 80

million species live in rainforests. As many as 6,000 species are forever lost every year because of logging. ☞Many other species around the world are endangered, mostly due to human activity, such as building roads and cities. Some are threatened because we consider them valuable or attractive. Elephants are killed for their tusks; whales are hunted for the oils in their flesh. Some plants are threatened when they are taken from the wild and sold to plant lovers. If these species are not protected, they can become extinct—that is, they will disappear forever. Extinction is natural—since the beginning of time, millions of species have disappeared. But since humans appeared on earth (we are relative latecomers), the rate of extinction has speeded up.

AMAZING FACT

A plant called the rosy periwinkle, which grows in the rainforests of Madagascar, has been used to make a drug that can cure some kinds of cancer.

WHAT CAN YOU DO?

First, you can encourage your parents not to buy furs, ivory, corals, and other products made from endangered species. You can also avoid certain pets that were bred in captivity. Later on, we'll provide details on how to adopt an endangered animal, and other ways to get involved.

Too Much Trash

How many things will you throw away today? An empty cereal box? Your lunch bag? An empty soda can? Some papers from school? When you stop and think about it, you may be surprised at how much trash you toss out.

Every year, the typical American family throws out:

- ☞ 2,460 pounds of paper
- ☞ 540 pounds of metals
- ☞ 480 pounds of glass
- ☞ 480 pounds of food scraps

All told, each of us throws away more than 1,200 pounds of trash per year, far more than people in most other countries. About 80 percent of that garbage ends up in landfills—dumps, as they are more commonly known. (Of the remaining 20 percent, about half is recycled and half is incinerated.) One big problem is that we are running out of landfill space—more than half of the

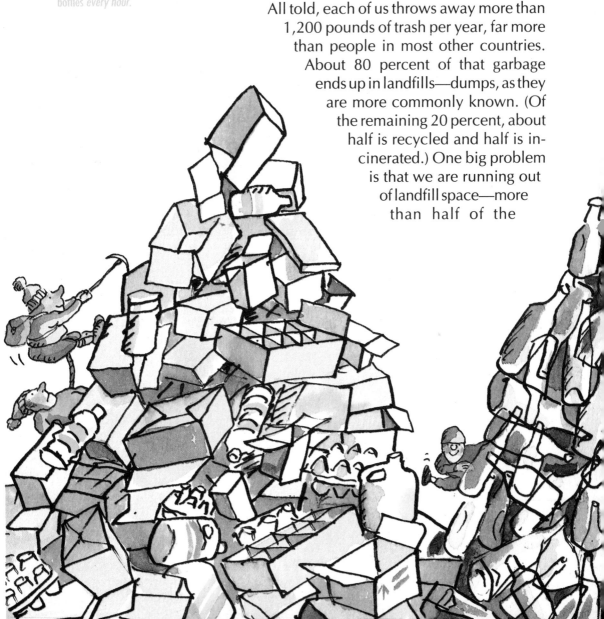

nation's landfills will be full within ten years.

Where will we put all our garbage when we've run out of space?

But trash presents more than a space problem. Between 5 and 15 percent of what we throw away contains hazardous substances—substances that can seep into the ground and contaminate air, water, and soil, eventually injuring people and other living things. Batteries, plastics, inks used on packages, and disposable diapers are just some of the things we throw away that contain hazardous substances that can cause serious problems.

THE PROBLEM OF PACKAGING

One of the things we throw away most often is packaging. Think about the products you and your family buy. From snack foods to compact discs, many products contain a great deal of packaging. Some have four or five layers, including several layers of plastic, far more than may be necessary. If your household is typical, about one-third

of the packaging you buy will be thrown away immediately upon opening a package.

Some packaging is important—it protects products and ensures hygiene—but a lot of packaging is there simply to catch our eye, to make us buy this product rather than that one. Excessive packaging also adds to the cost of a product, so you pay extra for products that have a lot of packaging. We also pay for garbage in other ways— through higher taxes needed to create new landfills, for example, and through higher medical bills and health insurance costs required to cure the illnesses caused by pollution.

THE RECYCLING SOLUTION

The real tragedy behind the mountains of trash we produce is that a lot of what we throw away can be reused or recycled.

Not everything is recyclable, and some materials are more easily recycled than others. But recycling makes perfect sense in any case. After all, why throw away what we can reuse?

What exactly can be recycled? Amost anything:

☛ **Metals**—such as aluminum, steel, and tin. All of these metals must be mined from the ground, which can damage the local landscape and create water

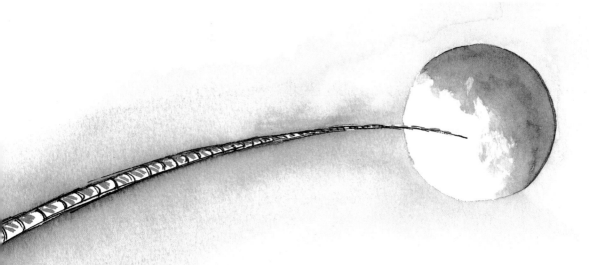

and air pollution. Most metals can be melted down and recycled again and again. This saves huge amounts of energy.

☞ **Glass**—is made largely from sand, and there is hardly a shortage of that in the world. However, turning the sand into glass takes a large amount of energy. Much less energy (and much less sand) is used when glass is melted down and made into new bottles and jars. Every ton of crushed waste glass used saves the equivalent of about 30 gallons of oil.

☞ **Paper**—is made from trees, of course, and cutting down trees can cause environmental problems. In the United States we cut down more than 4 billion trees a year to make paper and cardboard for newspapers, magazines, packaging, junk mail, kitchen towels, toilet paper, boxes (and homework assignments!), among many other things. It takes at least 25 years for a tree to grow tall enough to be made into paper—which we may use and throw away in a matter of minutes! Turning trees into paper also uses tremendous amounts of energy and water and causes a great deal of air and water pollution.

☞ **Plastics**—are made from chemicals, many of which are made of fossil fuels such as oil. Because the technology has not been perfected, very little plastic is being recycled in the United States. And recycling plastic is different from recycling glass, aluminum, and paper. While you can turn used paper into new paper, and turn an aluminum can

AMAZING FACT

Eighty-four percent of a typical household's waste—including food scraps, yard waste, paper, cardboard, cans, and bottles—can be recycled.

or glass bottle into another can or bottle, you cannot turn a plastic hamburger container into another container. At best, that container can be made into something different—a flowerpot, for example, or a videocassette box—so there are limits to the usefulness of recycling plastic.

☛ **Other materials**—this includes a variety of products that we use every day, such as batteries (including automobile batteries), clothing, oil, tires, and yard wastes. Later in this book, we'll give specific suggestions on how to recycle some of these things.

What *can't* be recycled? In general, it isn't possible to recycle things made out of several different kinds of material—several kinds of plastics, for example, or metals mixed with plastic or paper. Here are just three examples of unrecyclable things guaranteed to end up in landfills:

☛ aerosol cans, made from several kinds of metals and plastics.

☛ juice boxes, made from a combination of plastic, cardboard, and aluminum foil.

☛ squeezable plastic ketchup (and mustard and other products) bottles, made from several different kinds of plastic molded together.

THE MYTH OF DEGRADABILITY

We used to think that after we discarded something into a landfill that it would eventually biodegrade—that is, it would rot and disappear completely. But we have come to learn that this doesn't really happen.

In a sense, everything in the world is biodegradable. Given enough time, air, sunlight, and other elements, your family's house, car, and possessions will all break down and wear away. It could take hundreds or even thousands of years for this to occur, but it will happen sooner or later.

But when things are buried in a landfill, where there is little if any air or sunlight, things do not break down. In fact, burying things in a landfill tends to *preserve* trash rather than *dispose* of it!

HOW TO TELL WHAT'S RECYCLED

There are several ways to identify products made of recycled material. Some products state on their labels "Made of recycled material." But some labels don't disclose *how much* of the material is recycled. Is it 5 percent or 100 percent? There may be no way of knowing.

Look for the recycled symbol to the right. But be careful: sometimes the symbol means that the product *can be recycled*, not that it is made from recycled material.

If the product or package is made from cardboard, such as a box of cereal or crackers, there is an easy way to tell whether it has been recycled. Peak under the top flap. If the *underside* of the cardboard is gray or dark brown, the box is made from recycled material. If the underside is white, it is made from virgin (unrecycled) material.

Whenever you have a choice, always choose the product made from recycled material.

You have probably read or heard about the ancient Egyptians, who buried their leaders by wrapping them tightly in cloth and placing them in boxes stored in cool, dark places—mummies. Burying trash in landfills works in a similar way.

So, counting on trash to break down (sometimes referred to as biodegradability or photodegradability) is not a solution to our mountains of trash.

WHAT CAN YOU DO?

You probably already know about the "three Rs"—reading, 'riting, and 'rithmatic. But there are three more Rs you should know to help you become a Green Consumer:

> ☞ **Refuse** to buy things that are excessively packaged, that are made of plastics or other materials that are not fully recyclable, that are wasteful in other ways, or that you don't really need.
>
> ☞ **Reuse** whatever you can. (We'll give more specific suggestions later on.) And buy products made of or packaged in reused (recycled) material.
>
> ☞ **Recycle** as much as you can. (Again, we'll give specific suggestions later on.) This allows us to get the most use out of our precious resources.

So, let's put it all together. As you begin to look at the individual environmental problems, you will begin to see how many of them are related. You will also begin to see some common solutions. For example:

- ☛ Acid rain, global warming, and air pollution all result largely from automobiles and from the production of electricity in power plants. So, all three problems would be helped by driving cars more efficiently and by using energy wisely.
- ☛ The destruction of trees—whether in forests, cities, or rural areas—contributes to air pollution and global warming, as well as to the loss of plant and animal species. So, saving forests and planting trees can help ease all three problems.
- ☛ Some of the same materials containing ozone-destroying CFCs also contribute to the problem of too much trash. So, reducing use of Styrofoam coffee cups and fast-food containers, among other things, will help ease both problems.

As you can see, nearly everything on Earth is related. That is why every little bit that you can do helps. By becoming aware of even one environmental problem in your home, your school, or your community—and then doing something about it—you are contributing to improving the environment all over the world! That makes each of us a pretty powerful person.

Now you understand the basic problems. In the next section, we will help you to rate yourself, your family, your school, and your community to see how green each of them is. Armed with this knowledge, you will be ready to "go green."

How Green Are You?

Just about everything you do has an effect on the environment. That's true for you, your family, and everyone else. You can do things in a wasteful, polluting way, or in a resourceful, nonpolluting, "green" way.

In this section we'll show you how to conduct a Green Audit of your home, your school, and your community. Conducting your audit will require that you ask a lot of questions and do some investigations of your own. You may be surprised at what you find out!

—What Is a "Green Audit"? —

Simply put, an audit is an examination of something. Let's say you wanted to audit your refrigerator to determine exactly what foods are being eaten, by whom, and how often. You might start by taking an inventory of exactly what is in the refrigerator, then checking it a few hours later to see what has been eaten. You might interview others in your family to see who's eaten what. After a few days of doing this, you could come to some conclusions—that no one has touched the Swiss cheese in days, for example, or that the whole bottle of apple juice disappeared within a few hours of bringing it home from the store, or that your sister absolutely hates yogurt.

You can conduct an audit of just about anything. In this section, you will learn how to conduct a Green Audit of your home, your school, and your community. In the process, you will learn a great deal about the places in which you live and spend time, and how they may be contributing to some of the environmental problems we discussed in the previous section. Then you can start to do something about them.

Because your home, your school, and your community are unique, your Green Audit will probably be somewhat different from the ones we've described in the following pages. You needn't follow our audit exactly. You may come up with some of your own questions. The more questions you ask, the more you'll find out. You can conduct the audit by yourself or with one or more other people—your family, your friends, or your classmates.

Once you've finished your audit, you'll be well informed and ready to start taking some actions to make your world a greener one.

—How Green Is Your Home?—

Let's start with a look around your home. We'll begin in the room that's just about everyone's favorite—the kitchen—and move into other rooms, and then outside.

Try to answer the questions in this audit as thoroughly as possible. In many cases, you'll need to ask some questions—of your parents, perhaps, or even your electric utility company. You may want to start a Green Audit Logbook—a notebook with your findings, observations, and ideas. As the final step in your audit, you'll be asked to make some recommendations on how your home can be a greener one.

THOUGHT FOR FOOD: THE KITCHEN

In some homes, the kitchen is the center of activity. There's good reason for this: Everyone in your family has to eat, usually several times a day. And when you consider all the time that is spent shopping, cooking, and cleaning up (not to mention eating!), it's no wonder the kitchen is a busy place.

The kitchen is also the place where there's a lot you can do to make things greener.

1. The Pantry. If you've ever helped to unpack the shopping bags or noticed how quickly the garbage can fills up with empty boxes, bottles, and other things, you'll understand the problem of wasteful packaging. About half of the trash we throw away at home consists of this packaging—some of which we scarcely look at or use for more than a few seconds. Some products seem to have endless layers of packaging—a plastic tray with a plastic cover in a plastic bag in a cardboard box . . . that is wrapped in still more plastic!

Take a look along the kitchen shelves. How many examples of overpackaging can you spot? Look for items wrapped in several layers. Are all those layers really necessary? Make a list of the products you think could be just as good with less packaging.

One easy way to reduce the amount of packaging is to buy in bulk. Can you find anything on the kitchen shelves packed in a giant-sized container—breakfast cereal, for example, or those big bottles of juice or soda? A large package may contain three or four times as much as a small package, but without three or four times as much packaging.

2. Shopping Bags.

How does your family bring groceries home from the market? In shopping bags, probably. But what happens to those bags after the groceries are unpacked? Do you throw them out? Do heaps of plastic or paper bags fall out of the cupboard every time you open it? If so, someone in your family is probably bringing home a new grocery bag every time he or she goes shopping.

There's no need for this. You can reuse shopping bags by bringing them back to the grocery the next time you go shopping. Better still, you can use a cloth bag that will last for years (when it gets dirty, simply put it in the wash). Sometimes, when you are buying only one or two things, you may not need any bag at all. Tell the clerk at the store, "That's okay. I'll just carry it myself."

Over a two-week period, keep track of exactly how many grocery bags are brought into your home and what happens to them.

3. Trash.

While we're on the subject of throwing things away, let's take a look at how much kitchen trash your family throws away and exactly what's in that trash. Are you throwing away things that could be recycled? Are there materials in the trash that could be poisonous? Are there some things in the trash that could be reused before they are discarded?

Over the course of a week, go through five different bags of trash to determine how much of what's being thrown away could be reused or recycled.

You'll probably need some adult help for this, because this

investigation can create quite a mess. It also may be helpful to wear gloves and old clothes. Be careful about dangerous things like broken glass and sharp cans. And be prepared for things being a little bit smelly. Try to estimate how much of the trash is plastic, glass, aluminum, cardboard, newspapers, and food wastes. Think of ways the amount of trash your family produces can be reduced.

4. Fruits and Vegetables.
You probably don't think much about what is involved in getting your family's food onto the dinner table. The fact is, everything you eat needs energy to grow, to manufacture, to transport to the grocery store, and to cook. Consider this:

- ☞ Some foods use a lot of resources such as water and fertilizer. Because we have come to expect to have many types of produce available all year long, many common foods are imported from faraway states and foreign countries. It takes a great deal of energy—which creates pollution—to transport food by airplane, ship, and truck to your local market.
- ☞ A lot of foods are sprayed with pesticides while they are growing to get rid of insects and other pests. Sometimes, little bits of those chemicals—many of which are poisonous to people and animals—end up on the fruits and vegetables that you eat! Even something as healthy as an apple can make you sick if it contains pesticide residues. What's worse, these chemicals can also drain into our water supply, causing water pollution.

Some farmers, concerned about the effects of chemicals on the environment and on our food, have turned to "organic" farming methods. They don't use many chemical sprays—in fact, some use none at all! Organic farming was once used only by small family farms, but now organic methods are being used by some of the larger farms that supply some of the fruits and vegetables your family eats.

As a result, organic produce now can be found in supermarkets. Unfortunately, some people don't like organic produce because it is not as attractive as produce grown using non-organic methods. Some organic produce comes in a variety of shapes and colors, or has blemishes on the outside.

That's okay. Just as you can't judge a book by its cover, you can't judge produce by how pretty it is. Would you rather eat something pretty, or something that isn't as pretty but which tastes good and is better for your health and the environment?

Ask at a supermarket how their fruits and vegetables are grown. Do farmers use "organic" methods? What states and countries does the produce come from? Find out if there are markets that sell produce grown locally, using a minimum of chemicals.

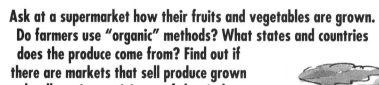

When you go to the store, take a look at how the produce is sold. Is it wrapped in plastic or other containers, or is it sold without any extra packaging? After all, why wrap an orange or apple in plastic or some other material when it already has its own natural packaging?

5. Meat and Poultry.

Not everyone eats meat. About 5 percent of Americans are vegetarians. Some vegetarians don't eat any meat or fish at all, while others eat fish and chicken but not "red" meats such as beef, lamb, and pork.

Producing all this meat—especially beef, from which hamburgers and steaks are made—takes a great deal of energy and resources, and generates a lot of pollution. For example:

- ☞ Producing one pound of beef takes 16 pounds of grain and soybeans (which are part of a cow's diet), 2,500 gallons of water, and the energy equivalent of a gallon of gasoline.
- ☞ More than half of all the water used in the United States is used for raising livestock.
- ☞ More than 200 million acres of land in the U.S. have been deforested to raise livestock. In the tropical rainforests, about 27 million acres are permanently destroyed each year, mostly to raise beef that is exported to North America.
- ☞ Chicken farming can be polluting, too. Chickens are fed antibiotics and laboratory-created food, none of which is good for the environment—or for you.

Keep track of how many meat and poultry meals you and your family eat during a one-week period, both at home and away from home.

Consider occasionally eating a vegetarian meal—one that has no meat. Cutting down on the amount of meat and poultry you eat is not only healthy for you, it is good for the Earth.

You should also take a look at the packages in which your family's meat, poultry, and dairy products are sold. For example, does your family buy milk in plastic jugs instead of cardboard containers? Are eggs purchased in plastic foam containers instead of cardboard ones? Does cheese come in individually wrapped slices instead of in one big chunk?

Is meat and poultry packed in foam trays and covered by plastic instead of wrapped in butcher paper? As you examine these purchases, you may want to go back and revise the list of overpackaged products you created on page 29.

6. Fish and Seafood. Fish and seafood are very healthy and popular foods. They are low in fat and high in protein. But because the environments in which they live—rivers, bays, and oceans—often are not very clean, some fish aren't healthy to eat. In fact, because many pollutants can accumulate in a fish's fatty tissues, an individual fish can contain more pollutants than the water in which it is caught! To make things worse, the federal government does not inspect seafood for cleanliness the way it inspects meat and poultry.

Another problem is that some tuna are caught using huge nets that also trap dolphins. (Tuna, for some reason, swim just below herds of dolphins.) Each year, thousands of dolphins are killed or wounded by tuna fishermen. As

the Earth Island Institute puts it: "Dolphins aren't fish. They're mammals like us. They breathe air. They nurse their young. They communicate and work together in groups. Graceful and intelligent creatures, dolphins have been known to come to the aid of drowning humans."

Fortunately, some tuna companies have decided to catch only tuna caught in ways that don't harm dolphins. So if your family buys tuna, make sure the can indicates that it is "dolphin friendly," or words to that effect.

At the fish counter at a supermarket, ask whether the fish sold there have been inspected by the federal government for cleanliness. At home, check to see whether your family has bought cans of tuna that do not say it is "dolphin friendly."

7. Beverages.   What do you drink? If your family is typical, it consumes about 182 gallons of soda a year in addition to 29 gallons of juice, 104 gallons of milk, and 26 gallons of bottled water. That's a lot of bottles, cans, cartons, and jugs—and a lot of waste!

Let's look at the typical containers:

☞ Aluminum cans can be recycled. In fact, you can receive a few cents for every can you return to a recycling center. That can add up to a lot of money! You can usually identify an aluminum can by the rounded sides on the top and bottom, and by how easily you can squish an empty can with your bare hands. If you're not sure, use a magnet— an aluminum can will *not* stick to a magnet.

☞ Glass bottles also can be recycled. They can be

returned to nearly any recycling center.

☛ Plastic bottles usually cannot be easily recycled. While most soda bottles are made from a plastic called PET (it stands for "polyethylene terephthalate"), which can be recycled in limited ways, there are very few places you can take empty PET bottles for recycling.

☛ Individual juice boxes (the kind that come with their own insertable straw) are not recyclable because they are made from several layers of materials that cannot be separated when they are thrown away.

Take a look at the beverage containers you and your family buy during one full week. How many of them can be recycled easily? Of those that are recyclable, how many of them are actually being recycled by members of your family?

Does your family drink bottled water? A growing number of families do, sometimes because they feel that their tap water is not very clean, or because they believe bottled water has more minerals than tap water. But there are no laws that say bottled water must be cleaner than tap water. Some companies even get their water right out of the tap before putting it in bottles!

It takes a great deal of energy to transport millions of gallons of water around the country, some of which originates overseas. And bottled water creates a great deal of trash in the form of glass and plastic jugs. So bottled water is not a particularly "green" product.

8. Food Wraps and Paper Towels.

What do you do with leftovers? You probably wrap them in aluminum foil or plastic wrap. These are okay if you use them sparingly, and if you recycle and reuse them whenever possible. Aluminum foil can be recycled along with your soda cans. Plastic wrap cannot be recycled, so it should be used only when absolutely necessary.

Don't forget about reusable plastic containers. They make excellent storage devices. You can buy these in stores, but they also come with many deli salads, carry-out foods, and other products. Instead of throwing them away, they can be washed and used over and over!

Do you use a microwave oven? If so, use wax paper instead of plastic wrap to cover dishes while they heat. Not only does it break down easier than plastic wrap when disposed of, wax paper also reduces the chance of your getting burned when you take a hot dish out of the oven.

What about paper towels? The "greenest" thing is to not use them at all, choosing a cloth towel instead. But if you must use them, choose a brand made from 100 percent recycled fiber. You probably can't tell the difference between these towels and the ones you're used to—but the trees sure can! Also, avoid brands that contain dyes and inks that can pollute the water.

Check to see what kinds of food wraps and paper towels your family usually uses, and whether there are reusable containers available that can cut down the amount of food wrap being used.

UNDER THE SINK: CLEANING SUPPLIES

A great deal of cleaning goes on in most homes. We wash, scrub, vacuum, spray, and polish so that we may keep our homes clean and neat. Strange as it may seem, some of these cleaners also can cause pollution, both indoors and outdoors. Let's take a look at some of the most common cleaning supplies in your home to see how green they are.

1. Laundry detergent. Your washer sends a lot of dirty water down the drain. But what's in that water—besides dirt, that is?

Many detergents contain *phosphates*, chemicals that help get clothes clean. But when phosphates get into waste water, they speed the growth of algae, a plant that grows in the water. Too much algae can kill fish, plants, and other things that live in the water.

In addition to phosphates, many detergents contain concentrated chemicals, including *surfactants* (which help with the cleaning) and *bleach* (which removes stains and stops white clothes from turning yellow). One problem with surfactants is that they are made from petroleum, the nonrenewable resource from which oil and gasoline are made.

Read the labels. Some detergents claim to be "biological," meaning that they contain enzymes that help to dissolve stains and make the detergent work in cooler water. Some detergents claim to be "biodegradable," an overused term that suggests that the detergent breaks down and becomes harmless in the waste system. But this doesn't always happen.

The important thing to know is that more and more manufacturers are putting useful information about their ingredients on their packages.

Speaking of packages, how is your laundry detergent packaged? Does it come in a hard plastic jug—which may not be recycled easily—or does it come in a recycled cardboard box? (See page 25 for information on how to tell whether a box is made of recycled cardboard.)

Examine the laundry detergent your family buys. Note whether it contains phosphates or other harmful ingredients and whether it comes in a plastic or cardboard container.

2. Other Cleaners. Many cleaners contain ingredients that are harmful when they go down the drain or when they get into the air. For example:

☞ **All-purpose cleaners** contain ammonia, which can be

harmful to the lungs, and chlorine, which can form cancer-causing compounds when released into the environment.

☞ **Bleach** is a strong chemical used to kill germs in sinks, drains, and toilets. Most bleach contains cancer-causing chlorine. If you have a septic tank, bleach also kills the useful bacteria that help the sewage to decompose.

☞ **Drain cleaners** contain very strong chemicals such as lye and hydrochloric and sulfuric acids. These can burn your skin and can cause blindness if they get in your eyes.

☞ **Flea and tick control products** contain ingredients that have never been adequately tested for safety. While not intended for use on people, they can rub off your pet and onto furniture, exposing you and others to the risk of cancer and other diseases.

☞ **Floor and furniture polishes** contain phenol, which causes cancer in laboratory animals. Ingesting just one thimbleful can make you very, very sick.

☞ **Metal polishes** contain ammonia and phosphoric and sulfuric acids, which are not healthy to breathe.

☞ **Mothballs** contain p-dichlorobenzene, which causes cancer.

☞ **Oven cleaners** contain lye, a powerful chemical that can burn your skin and lungs or cause blindness if splashed in your eyes.

☞ **Toilet cleaners** contain chlorine and hydrochloric acid, which can burn your skin and eyes.

Another problem is packaging. For example, some cleaners come in aerosol sprays, which contain ingredients that contribute to air pollution. In addition, aerosol cans cannot be recycled. There are almost always alternatives to aerosol products, including pump sprays, liquids, and powders. Other products come in plastic bottles that cannot easily be recycled and which take up a lot of space in landfills. Many of these kinds of products are also available in glass bottles, which can be recycled.

Take a look at the cleaning products your family uses. Note which ingredients they contain that may be harmful. Also, determine whether any of the products are overpackaged or come in unre-cycled or unrecyclable containers.

We didn't always have all these hazardous cleaners. The products available when your parents were growing up were much simpler. In fact, many of the "old-fashioned" cleaners consisted of common ingredients your family probably has in its pantry—soap, borax, cornstarch, vinegar, and baking soda, for example. There are many books available that give simple recipes for making your own, nontoxic, nonpolluting household cleaning products.

MINDING YOUR WASTE: THE BATHROOM

Although you use the bathroom several times a day, you may not realize just how much it has to do with the environment. As you continue your Green Audit, here are some things to think about the way you and your family use this very personal place.

1. Baths and Showers. Which do you think uses more water—a bath, in which you fill the tub just once, or a shower, in which you let the water run and run? You may

be surprised at the answer: A bath can use up to twice as much water as a shower!

Why is saving water important? There are several reasons. When you use more water, you increase the amount of waste water that goes down the drain, which causes your local water-treatment plant to work extra hard to clean all that water. So, by reducing water use, you put less dirty water into the system. In addition, some areas don't have enough water to meet the needs of the growing population. You may already have experienced a drought in your area, during which your family had to restrict the amount of water it used.

Another reason for reducing water use—especially water used for bathing—is that by using less hot water, you will save energy, and reduce the pollution created by electric-generating plants. Your family will also save money by using less energy.

One way to reduce the amount of water you use in the shower is by installing low-flow shower heads. These cause the shower to use less water, although you'd probably never know it. They are available at many hardware stores.

Using the table on page 17, determine how much water your family uses in showers and baths each week. Determine if there are ways to reduce the amount of water you use, including installing low-flow shower heads.

2. Leaky Faucets and Toilets. A drippy faucet may not seem like a big problem, but it adds up over time. Even a tiny leak can waste more than 3,000 gallons of water over

the course of a year. A leaky toilet can waste more than 20,000 gallons! According to one expert, about one out of every five toilets in the U.S. is leaking at this very moment.

A leaky faucet is easy to spot, but how do you know whether your toilet is leaking? Here's an easy test: First, remove the top of the toilet tank (you should probably check

AMAZING FACT

The typical American home uses about 300 gallons of water a day.

with your parents before doing this). Then, add a few drops of food coloring to the tank. Make sure that no one uses the toilet while this test is being conducted. After about 20 minutes, check the toilet bowl. If you see the colored water in the bowl, your toilet is leaking.

Fixing a leaky toilet or faucet is pretty simple. Your parents can buy an inexpensive kit at a hardware store that comes with instructions on what to do. You may even be able to do it yourself!

Check all the faucets and toilets in your home—including faucets located on the outside of the house—to see if there are any leaks. Make a list of possible leaks for later action.

3. Flushing the Toilet.

One third of the water used in most homes is flushed down the toilet. That's more than we use in any other part of our home. Every time you flush the toilet, between five and seven gallons of fresh water go down the drain. But there are ways to reduce that amount. The simplest way is to put something in the tank to reduce the amount of water it takes to fill it up after each flush.

You can buy a little plastic device called a "toilet dam" that will create a smaller space for water to have to fill. But you can also create your own low-flush system using an empty plastic jug—a gallon or half-gallon jug works best. (You should get your parents to help you with this.) If you fill the jug with water and replace the cap, and place it into the tank in a way that doesn't get in the way of the flushing mechanism, you'll save water with every flush!

Another thing you flush down the toilet is toilet paper. There are brands of toilet paper made from 100 percent recycled paper. It's a shame to cut down trees—just to have them flushed down the toilet. Also avoid brands that contain inks and dyes. They aren't necessary and they represent yet another kind of chemical flushed down the drain.

Determine how many toilets in your home could be fitted with a toilet dam or other device to save water. Also, check to see whether the toilet paper your family buys is made from recycled paper, or whether it contains unnecessary inks and dyes.

4. Soaps and detergents.
The plant oils and animal fats used to make most soaps and shampoos do not seriously pollute the water. However, the dyes and perfumes may take longer to biodegrade.

Be aware, however, that many personal care products—including soaps, deodorants, hair sprays, conditioners, and makeup—are tested on animals to determine whether they are safe for human use. Many of these tests cause animals to suffer and to die slow, torturous deaths. For that reason, a growing number of personal-care-product companies have begun using alternative testing methods that don't cause animals to suffer. Look for these products—they usually state on the package that they are "cruelty free."

Also, be on the lookout for overpackaging of these products. Many personal care products and cosmetics—especially those intended for use by girls and women—have lots of wasteful packaging. Aerosols, as we said earlier, are wasteful, and there are almost always alternative products available.

Check to see whether the soaps and other personal care products your family uses are "cruelty free," and whether they come in wasteful packages or containers.

5. Brushing Your Teeth.
You can save even more water by turning off the faucet when you brush. There's simply no need to keep the water running the whole time you brush. You could be wasting up to five gallons of water with each brushing!

Also, avoid wasteful "pump" toothpaste dispensers. These may be easier to use, but they create a great deal of unnecessary waste. Some toothpaste containers are now made of aluminum, which can be recycled along with cans and foil.

Find out if members of your family keep the water running when they brush, and whether they use toothpaste in pumps instead of tubes.

There are probably other things you can do in the bathroom to save water and energy. If you or your parents shave, for example, avoiding disposable razors is a must! And avoid shaving cream packaged in aerosol cans.

ENERGY EATERS: HOUSEHOLD APPLIANCES

The many machines around your home all run on electricity. (The exception is your heating system, which may operate on oil or natural gas.) The appliances that heat or cool (stove, iron, water heater, clothes dryer, refrigerator, light bulbs) or have moving parts (washing machine, dishwasher) use a lot more energy than those that don't (clock, television, radio).

In addition, large amounts of energy are used to manufacture all these appliances, not to mention transporting them to your local store.

So, it makes sense to make the most of every appliance your family buys. That means buying products that use the least amount of energy, and which will last the longest amount of time.

1. Energy Efficiency.

You may be surprised to learn which appliances in your home guzzle the most electricity. You may have been taught to always turn off the lights when you leave the room. That's good advice, but lights are only part of the problem. Your refrigerator, for example, quietly gurgling away in the corner of the kitchen, has a far bigger electrical appetite.

Energy-efficient appliances sometimes cost more to purchase than other appliances, but the purchase price is deceiving. When you look at the *life-cycle costs*—the purchase price of an appliance plus the cost of operating

it during its lifetime—energy-efficient appliances can cost hundreds of dollars less! That's because you save money each year in reduced electricity costs. Over the 15- or 20-year life of an appliance, those savings can really add up.

Federal law requires that many major appliances be sold with energy-efficiency labels, giving estimates of how much it will cost to operate the appliance each year. Reading the labels makes it easy to choose the most efficient appliances.

Ask your parents if they know the energy efficiency ratings of their appliances. If your family is considering buying a new appliance, find out if there are ratings that can help you choose the most efficient models.

2. Using Appliances.

Of course, how you use your appliances also makes a big difference in how much energy they consume. For example:

- ☛ When you boil water on a stove, leave the lid on the pot.
- ☛ Leave the oven door closed when baking to keep the heat from escaping.

☞ Use a microwave oven only for cooking, not for defrosting.

☞ Use a clothes washer or dishwasher only with a full load, and at the coolest water setting possible.

☞ When you open the refrigerator, close it as quickly as possible so that you don't lose much cool air.

3. Light Bulbs. Did you notice that we earlier referred to light bulbs as "appliances"? They're not exactly like refrigerators or clothes dryers, but they still serve a similar purpose: to provide you with comfort and convenience. Just imagine how different life would be without light bulbs!

Just as with other appliances, it is important to buy the most energy-efficient bulbs. The least-efficient are called "incandescents"—these are the screw-in bulbs you probably have in your lamps and ceiling fixtures. These are inefficient because 90 percent of the energy they use is given off as heat instead of light. That's a lot of waste!

Fluorescent bulbs—usually in the form of long tubes that take an extra second or two to come on when you flip the switch—are much more energy efficient and last a lot longer, but they are not practical for many purposes because of their size and shape. Besides, a lot of people don't like the kind of light given off by these fluorescents.

A new kind of bulb—called "compact fluorescents"—provides a lot more light for a lot less energy. Although these are fluorescents, they can screw into most fixtures and use about one-fourth the energy of incandescents. Even better, they last ten times longer than most incandescents! They also give off a much more pleasant light that traditional fluorescents.

Compact fluorescents cost more than incandescents, but as we said before, the cost of buying any appliance is only a fraction of what it will cost to operate over its lifetime. So, compact fluorescents will save money over time because they use less energy and last longer.

Find out how many of your home's light bulbs could be replaced by compact fluorescents. Ask your parents to consider buying compact fluorescents the next time they need to replace a bulb.

4. Heating and Cooling.

About half of the energy used in your home is spent on heating and cooling it. It takes a lot of electricity, oil, and natural gas to run all the furnaces, heaters, air conditioners, and heat pumps, and that creates a lot of pollution. So, the more that a heater or air conditioner must operate, the greater the costs and pollution. The idea, then, is to heat and cool as little as possible.

But that doesn't mean you have to be too cold or too hot. If your home is properly insulated, and if you take certain other steps, you'll stay comfortable and cut pollution at the same time!

Here's what you need to look for:

☞ Your **hot water heater** takes cold water and heats it. During times that you aren't using much hot water (while you are sleeping, for example) it must keep the hot water hot. If the water heater is insulated, it will take less energy to keep the water hot. Check to see if your hot water heater is insulated.

☞ Similarly, the **hot water pipes** that lead from the hot water heater to your sink or shower also should be insulated.

☞ If you have a **furnace**, it should be checked and cleaned at least once a year. If it has air filters, they should be cleaned or changed several times a year. Dirty filters make the furnace work harder and use more energy to produce the same amount of heat. Find out when the filters were last cleaned.

- ☞ Your **air conditioners** also have filters, and they should be cleaned, too.
- ☞ Of course, you can save energy by turning down the **thermostat** in winter and turning it up in summer. If it is winter, check to see that the thermostat is generally set no higher than 68° Fahrenheit. If it is summer, check to see that it is set no lower than 72° Fahrenheit.
- ☞ A lot of energy can escape through the **windows**. When it's cold, you can reduce the escaping heat by pulling down the shades or closing the curtains. If any windows are cracked, they should be fixed.
- ☞ Energy also escapes through **leaks** around windows and doors. On a cold day, you can detect the leaks by placing a piece of paper or a ribbon around the windows and doors; if it moves, you've found a leak! Tell your parents right away! The leak should be plugged with caulk or other material.

Make a survey of your home's heating and cooling use to see if it could be made more efficient. Make suggestions on how your household could be made more energy efficient.

Your local utility may conduct an energy inspection for free or may provide detailed information on how you can do it. You may also get ideas about things you can do from a clerk at a local hardware store. Just like with energy-efficient appliances, some of the energy-reducing measures may cost a little money, but they will more than pay for themselves eventually through energy cost savings. And your household will create less pollution, too.

A HOME WITHIN YOUR HOME: YOUR ROOM

Some people have big bedrooms with lots of room to play or listen to music or conduct science experiments or whatever. Others have smaller bedrooms they share with someone else, but use a different room for playing or visiting or just hanging out. Whatever you consider to be "your" room, you probably don't think of it as an environmental problem. But let's take a closer look.

1. Clothing and Fashion.   You've probably noticed that some of your clothes feel different from others. That's  because they are made of different materials. Some of the materials are natural because they come from plants and animals. These include wool, cotton, and fur. Other materials are synthetics, meaning that they are manufactured from chemicals and other ingredients. Examples of synthetics are polyester, acrylic, rayon, and nylon. The labels of your clothes should tell you from which materials they are made, but it is difficult to say which is the "greenest" material because there are problems with *all* of them! None is entirely environmentally friendly. As a general rule, though, we recommend natural rather than synthetic fibers, because most synthetic fibers are made from oil.

Here are some of the things you should check for in your Green Audit:

☞ **Animal Furs** encourage the killing of animals, including several endangered species, many of which experience pain and suffering in the process. Even "fake" furs made of synthetic materials still encourage the killing and wearing of animals. Environmentalists consider fake furs to be nearly as bad as the real ones. Besides, fake furs are made from oil-based fibers, which are nonrenewable resources.

☞ **Ivory** from elephant tusks is responsible for killing between 200 and 300 African elephants *every day*. At that rate, the species could be extinct within 20 years. By purchasing—or even wearing—ivory, no matter how small, you are encouraging the slaughter of elephants.

☞ **Tortoiseshell, reptile skins, and coral** are three more things that come from endangered species. Tortoises, reptiles, and turtles are threatened in many parts of the world. Coral comes from reefs, which are homes to millions of plants and creatures. But they are beginning to disappear, partly because they are being polluted and partly to make jewelry and other ornaments.

☞ **Shells** are fun to collect, but in the process you should make sure you are not being an environmental vandal. Picking up empty shells from the beach is fine because they are dead. But buying exotic shells and trinkets made from them from shell shops often means that living creatures were plucked from the ocean for this purpose.

Check to see if you or anyone in your family has clothing or jewelry made from animal fur or an endangered species. If so, encourage them not to wear these articles, and not to buy other articles made of such materials.

2. Recycling Clothes (and other things).
Just because you can no longer use something you own doesn't mean it loses its value. If you've outgrown something, or it has gone out of style, it may still be useful to someone else. Throwing something away is a waste of the materials

and energy it took to manufacture it. Besides, you can do any of the following with clothing—as well as toys, books, furniture, appliances, and other things you no longer need or want:

- ☞ You can donate them to a charity. (Your parents may get a tax deduction for this.)
- ☞ You can sell them at a yard or garage sale and earn some extra money.
- ☞ You can offer them to a homeless person on the street.

You may also consider holding on to outdated fashions— you never know when they'll come back into style!

3. Batteries.   Americans throw away 2^1/$_2$ *billion* batteries every year. But batteries contain high levels of mercury, a poisonous metal, and mercury from discarded batteries pollutes the water.

There are two things you can do. Some things can be powered by solar electricity—light. Solar-powered calculators and watches, for example, eliminate the need for batteries altogether! If you do need batteries, buy rechargeable ones. When they wear out, they can be inserted into a box called a recharger, and made as good as new. That way, you can reuse batteries over and over.

Some day, batteries will be recyclable. Until then, use them wisely.

AROUND THE HOUSE

As you continue your Green Audit, here are some of the other things you should check:

1. Hazardous Wastes.   Is your basement filled with old cans of paint, oil, or solvents? When it comes time to dispose of them, make sure that they are thrown away properly. *Do not throw them in the trash!* They should be brought to a hazardous waste collection site in your community. (Call your city of county office to find the location of the nearest site.) Many service stations accept used motor oil and some other materials.

Check to see if there are hazardous substances being stored in or around your home. If so, make sure they are disposed of properly.

2. Pesticides.   Does your home have a garden? Gardening is one of the most popular hobbies in the United States. But many pesticides used in gardens and on lawns are very poisonous—not just to people, but also to birds, animals, and to soil and water. Some of the pesticides used on home gardens can cause cancer.

Many people grow beautiful gardens and lawns without using a lot of pesticides, using "organic" or "low-impact" gardening methods. You or your parents might consider buying or borrowing at a library one of the many books that describe ways to garden without pesticides.

Check to see what pesticides are being used in and around your home. Find out if there are less toxic alternatives. If you have a gardener or lawn-care service, ask what kind of pesticides they use, and whether they offer alternative, low-impact services.

3. Car Care.   If your parents have a car, it should be kept

in good shape so that it gets the most miles for every gallon of gas. Automobiles are one of the most polluting things in our society. They contribute to air pollution, acid rain, global warming, ozone depletion, water pollution, and disappearing landfills.

Keeping a car in shape—and driving it properly—are the best ways to minimize the polluting effects of cars. Here are some things to check for:

- When was the car last tuned? It should be tuned every 6,000 to 7,500 miles. That includes having the filters cleaned, checking the tire pressure, changing the oil, and adjusting the alignment.
- Does the car have radial tires? Radials offer better gas mileage than other tires.
- Is the car used for short trips? Shorter trips can use more gas than longer ones. Combine several errands at once, or walk, bike, or take the bus.
- Are speed limits observed? Driving fast wastes gas.
- Is the car driven with the air conditioner on? That makes the car use more gas, too. However, driving with all the windows open also uses a lot of gas.
- Do your parents use the lowest-octane gas recommended by the manufacturer? High-octane gases are polluting and expensive.

Find out how well the car is maintained, and talk with your parents and other drivers in your family about how their driving habits may waste gas and increase pollution.

4. Pets.   Do you have a dog or cat? Make sure you aren't using flea and tick killers that may also be poisoning your pet. There are several less dangerous ways to avoid or get rid of fleas and ticks, including adding brewer's yeast to your pet's diet. Also, bathing your dog or cat regularly helps get rid of these pests.

Do you have another kind of pet? Be careful it is not an exotic or endangered species. Some turtles, birds, and fish are badly treated when they are captured. The

Humane Society urges us not to buy tropical birds for pets.

If you must get rid of a pet, do so properly. A dog, cat, or bird should be given to a responsible home or animal shelter. Don't flush fish or other pets down the toilet. If you are unsure what to do, call a pet store.

Find out if there are alternatives to the pesticides you are using on your pet, or whether your pet might be of an endangered species.

COMPILING YOUR GREEN AUDIT

Now it's time to put together all the information you have gathered. Review your findings (did you put them in a Green Audit Logbook?) and come to some conclusions. Be sure to share them with other members of your family, and with your teacher and classmates. Then make a list of steps that should be taken to make your home greener. For example, you might decide to start

- ☛ buying products in bulk and with less packaging
- ☛ buying recycled paper towels
- ☛ using a phosphate-free laundry detergent
- ☛ fixing leaky faucets
- ☛ using a low-flow shower head and installing a toilet dam
- ☛ switching to compact fluorescent light bulbs
- ☛ cleaning your air conditioner's filters
- ☛ making sure the car is well tuned and the tires filled
- ☛ using a less toxic flea powder on your dog

The list can be as long as you want. The point is, try to cover as many subjects as possible. And make suggestions that you think members of your family will actually do.

Now, let's move on to your school.

— *How Green Is Your School?* —

If you and your family can do so much to help solve problems such as acid rain and the greenhouse effect, imagine how powerful hundreds of young green consumers could be if they worked together at school. If this happened at every school, the results would be dramatic!

"Greening" your school—whether in the choice of paper you use or in the way school meals are prepared—is a step-by-step process. The first step is to conduct a Green Audit. That will help you determine what changes can be made. So, now you can give your school a test, instead of the other way around!

In conducting your school audit, you'll need to ask many questions of the adults in the school as well as some of your fellow classmates. Don't be discouraged if people don't know the answers to some of your questions. It is valuable to discover how many people who *should* know what is going on around them, don't. Also, your questions may spark their interest in helping to protect the Earth.

In many schools, decisions about such things as which cleaners to use or how the food is prepared are not made by the principal but by the local school board. So, no one at the school may know, for example, whether the toilet paper used at your school is made of recycled material. And your school may not be able to change easily to a different brand, because all purchasing may be done by a central office.

Your audit will best be conducted by a group of students in cooperation with a teacher. Several classes could get involved, with each class investigating a separate area. Because every school is different, you needn't follow our audit exactly. You may come up with some of your own questions. (Some of the questions from the home audit might also apply to your school.) Remember that the more questions you ask, the more you'll find out.

Part of your plan should be to decide what to do with the audit when it is finished. It will be extremely useful to all sorts of people and they can learn a great deal from it. You could give copies to friends, other teachers and adults, members of the school board, and city and county officials. You should consider sending a copy to the local newspaper and television stations. You might also suggest that the school hold an assembly or other meeting at which you and others can talk about the audit.

One of the first things you want to find out is whether the school (or school district) has any environmental guidelines, or any individual at the school or the central office who is responsible for working to help the environment. The fact is, very few schools have either, but if yours does, getting the guidelines or in touch with the person in charge will be an important first step.

At the very least, inform your school's principal about what you are doing. He or she may be able to help you, or may provide access to people and places that can help you get the answers you need.

IN THE CLASSROOM

You probably don't realize how many different things you use in your classrooms over the course of a week. You use a lot of paper, of course, but what about other supplies? And are there other things going on in your classroom that may be wasting precious resources? Let's take a look.

1. Paper. How much paper do you use in class and for your homework? Include all kinds of paper except books—binder paper, drawing paper, class handouts, notebooks, newspapers, magazines, even tests! When you add up one week's worth of all the paper used by all of the students (and your teacher), it probably would make a nice big pile. You might actually try asking everyone to put their used paper in a pile for a week. Imagine what the pile would look like if everyone in your entire school added their paper!

Take a look at some of the paper that was thrown away. Is the paper used on both sides? Is some of the paper hardly used at all? Remember that it takes up to 15 years for a tree to grow big enough to be made into paper. Do you think that your class used those trees wisely? How could you have been less wasteful?

Try to figure out how much paper is used by your class during one typical week. See if you can calculate a whole school year's worth of paper. Then, try to estimate the paper use for the entire school for a whole year. Are there any ways you can think of to reduce the amount of paper?

2. Other Supplies. What else do you use at school? Try keeping a list of what you do at school for a whole week, what materials and supplies were used in the process, and whether they were used carefully and without waste. Include paints, pencils, glue, chalk, batteries, pens, calculators, bags, and anything else you can think of. (Don't include food-related things. We'll get to them in a moment.)

Take a look at what the supplies are made of. Some paints and crayons, for example, are made from petroleum. That means that you are coloring or drawing with valuable, nonrenewable resources! In addition, some of these art supplies contain chemicals such as *toluene* or *ethanol* that are not healthy to breathe.

There are many art supplies that use plants, vegetables, or beeswax to make their colors. Water-based paints, glues, and markers are much better for you and the Earth than oil-based ones.

When you are thinking about doing arts and crafts,

consider using recycled things in your projects. For example, empty egg cartons can make great paint holders. Old fabric and plastic can be used in your art, too. Try making a sculpture or collage out of things that might have otherwise been thrown away.

Take a look at all the supplies your class uses for a whole week. Determine whether there is any way to reduce waste, or to eliminate products that contain chemicals or petroleum products.

IN THE LUNCHROOM

You might first want to review the kitchen audit on pages 29–38 before going further. Your school probably has a kitchen, too—perhaps a very large one. So, in conducting your audit, you'll want to examine many of the same things you did at home:

- ☞ Does the kitchen purchase products that are wasteful or overpackaged?
- ☞ Are grocery bags, bottles, cans, and boxes recycled or reused?
- ☞ Is trash recycled?
- ☞ Do fruits or vegetables contain pesticide residues?
- ☞ Is canned tuna of the "dolphin-friendly" variety?
- ☞ What kinds of beverage containers are used?
- ☞ What kind of food wraps and paper towels are used?

You also might want to review the information on pages 45–47 to help you determine whether the kitchen uses energy-efficient appliances. Are gas stoves and ovens used? They are much more efficient than electrical appliances. Check to see if there are other parts of the kitchen in which energy-saving measures could be made.

What about the food that is served and the lunchroom itself? There are a variety of other things to consider:

☞ Is trash being discarded that could be recycled or reused? Look at all the recyclable materials: glass, paper, cardboard, aluminum, tin, even plastic. Are there receptacles in and around eating places where people can separate their trash before discarding it? If recycling isn't being done, how much needless waste do you estimate is being thrown away each week?

☞ Are leftovers and other food wastes recycled rather than simply thrown away? Is edible food given away to people who don't have enough to eat? Another use for unwanted food is compost. Your leftover peas could be used to help grow a beautiful flower garden!

☞ If your school has vending machines, examine the packaging of the products sold in them. Are there trash cans nearby for people to put their garbage?

What about people who *bring* their lunch? Try to figure out how many students do this. How is their food wrapped? Do they recycle the waste? How many individually wrapped items do they bring each day?

   Don't forget to include teachers in this exercise. (They may have their own lunchroom, which may include vending machines and cooking facilities.) After all, they eat lunch, too!

Conduct a careful examination of your school's eating facilities. Try to come up with a list of recommendations about how the school can use resources more efficiently and create less waste.

THE GROUNDS

Schools consist of more than just classrooms, lunchrooms, and other buildings. There are also playgrounds, parking lots, gardens, walkways, and other outdoor areas. Some schools have lots of trees and grassy areas, even lakes! You should examine all of these areas to see if there are things being done that are harming the Earth. For example:

☛ What pesticides, fertilizers, and other chemicals are used on the school grounds? Has the amount increased or decreased in the last few years? Are warning signs or other precautions taken to make sure that these substances don't harm people or animals? Are there safer alternatives available? Could some of them be eliminated?

☛ Does the school grow any fruits or vegetables? If so, are they grown organically? If there is no garden, is there room in which your class could grow an organic garden?

☛ Are there places on your school's grounds where trees could be planted to provide shade and reduce water erosion?

☛ How much water does the school use each year? Has this amount increased or decreased in the last few years? Does the school use low-flow or water-reducing devices on faucets and toilets? Does landscaping require significant amounts of water? Are there alternative plants that could survive with a lot less water?

☛ How much energy is used each year? Has this amount increased or decreased in the last few years? Has the school installed energy-saving devices such as compact-fluorescent light bulbs or energy-efficient appliances? Are the lights and heating (or air-conditioning) left on long after people have left the buildings? Are there other things that could be done to decrease energy use? What alternative sources of energy could be used?

☞ Does the school encourage birds, animals, and other safe wildlife to inhabit the trees and grassy areas? How many species of plants, animals, birds, and insects can you find on the grounds? Of the trees and shrubs, which ones are native to your area? (Those that aren't native often require more water and care than the others.)

Discuss these questions with your school's maintenance personnel, and do some inspections of your own, to answer these questions. Try to come up with as many specific recommendations as possible.

CLEANING AND MAINTENANCE

A school is a very busy place, and all those busy people get things dirty and create a lot of trash. Just like your home, the people who keep your school clean use a lot of different cleaning and maintenance supplies. You might want to review pages 38–41, which covers cleaning supplies at home, before you proceed with this part of your audit.

Some of the things you'll want to find out:

☞ Are there any cleaning supplies being used that may be causing environmental problems? Are there nontoxic alternatives available?

☞ Are cleaning supplies purchased in packages that are recyclable or made of recycled material? Does the school purchase supplies in the largest quantities possible to reduce the amount of packaging and the pollution from extra shipping?

☛ Does the school use paper towels and toilet paper made of recycled paper? If not, are such supplies readily available?

☛ How many pounds (or tons!) of trash does the school throw away each week? How much is that for a full school year? Are recycled materials such as glass, aluminum, and paper being separated and recycled? Are there ways to cut down on the amount of trash the school creates? Are there enough garbage cans and recycling bins around so that people can easily discard their trash without littering?

Interview the head of maintenance at your school to find out the answers to these questions. Consider conducting a survey of one representative trash can (see page 30) to determine whether there are specific improvements that could be made.

TRAFFIC AND TRANSPORTATION

You and your classmates probably make at least 400 trips to or from school each year. If you attend school for 12 years, that amounts to nearly 5,000 trips. If there are 400 teachers and students in your school, that's over *two million* trips! So, how everyone makes that trip is important. If each person is driven to school in a separate car, that will create a great deal of pollution. If many students walk, take the bus or are driven in car pools, your school will be responsible for creating a lot less pollution. So, you'll need to find out:

☛ How does each student and teacher get to and from school?

☛ Is there public transportation that could be better used to get people to school? Are bus stops close enough to school to make it easy to travel by bus?

☛ Do parents keep their car engines running while waiting to pick up their children?

- What is the average number of miles each car gets per gallon of gas? (You can get a rough estimate by asking 20 people at random how many miles per gallon their family's cars get, then adding the numbers and dividing by 20 to get an average.) How many gallons of gas are used during a whole school year?
- Is there a car pool system in place to connect people who have cars to those who need rides?
- Could school hours be changed slightly so that cars and buses won't need to sit in congested traffic on the way to school?

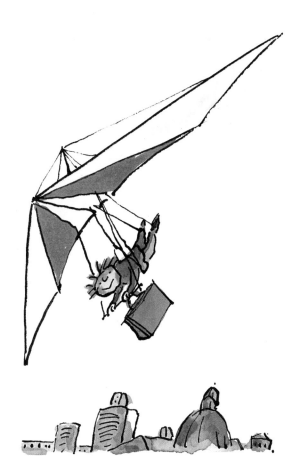

After you survey your school's transportation needs, try to come up with some specific suggestions about how it could be less polluting.

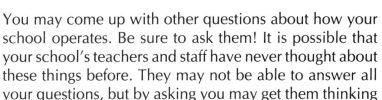

You may come up with other questions about how your school operates. Be sure to ask them! It is possible that your school's teachers and staff have never thought about these things before. They may not be able to answer all your questions, but by asking you may get them thinking about some important issues!

After you have asked all the questions, sit down and carefully review the information you've received. Try to make as many detailed suggestions as possible. Let your imagination run wild! Think of as many different ideas as you can to save energy, recycle materials, and reduce pollution. Who knows, one of your wildest ideas might just work!

As we said earlier, your school audit will have the most impact if you share it with the people in charge of your school and your school district, and with local newspapers and TV stations. Maybe you'll be on the 5 o'clock news!

How Green Is Your Community?

Just as you conducted a Green Audit of your home and your school, you can also audit your community to see how "green" it is.

What exactly is a "community"? It depends. For some people it may be a neighborhood. For others it may be a small town or part of a city. For still others, it may be an entire metropolitan area of a million or more people. In conducting your audit, you should choose whatever size "community" you can easily investigate. Don't take on a bigger area than you can handle.

As with your school audit, you will be more successful if you conduct this audit with a group— a class at school, perhaps, a scout troop, church group, a community or-

ganization, or any other group to which you belong.

If you already have conducted a school audit, you probably are familiar with how to ask good questions of people in charge so that you get the answers you need. That is equally important here. To get the information will require that you call or write a lot of very busy people in your area. Some of these people (or their assistants or secretaries) will gladly provide the information you need. Others will be less willing to provide information. So, be persistent!

When you complete your audit, you should share it with as many people as possible. Send copies to community leaders, heads of businesses, local newspapers and TV and radio stations, the mayor, the city council, and others who you think should know about your findings. As you did with the home and school audits, try to make your ideas and recommendations as specific as possible.

Every community is different, so we can't provide all the questions you should ask. Before you begin, talk with your parents, teachers, and others about their ideas on what parts of your community to audit. As you begin to ask questions, you probably will find other questions to ask. As we said before, don't hesitate to ask them!

TRAFFIC AND TRANSPORTATION

Are the streets in your community always full of traffic? If so, all those cars and trucks are wasting a lot of energy and creating a lot of pollution. There are many things communities can do to help ease traffic problems. Here are some of the things to find out:

☛ Are there enough buses and subways to help people get around easily? Could routes be changed easily to accommodate more people?

☛ Do major streets have bicycle lanes to make it easier and safer for people to ride bikes?

☛ Does the community encourage car pooling by setting up convenient pickup and drop-off sites?

☛ Are traffic signals timed to reduce the amount of time that cars are stopped at red lights?

☛ Are gas stations required to provide special devices on pumps to capture gas fumes, instead of releasing the fumes into the atmosphere to cause air pollution?

PARKS AND RECREATION AREAS

Your community probably has parks, pools, playgrounds, and other recreation areas. Review the section on auditing your school grounds (pages 63–65) for some of the things to look for. Other questions might include:

☛ Are there spaces for residents to plant vegetable or flower gardens?

☛ Is water used responsibly in gardens, fountains, lakes, and swimming pools?

☛ Is sufficient space provided in parks for birds, insects, animals, and other wildlife?

☛ Are plenty of trash cans around to reduce littering?

TRASH AND RECYCLING

As we learned before, there's a lot of things thrown away each day. How does your community take care of all the trash? You'll probably want to find out:

☞ Does the community offer curbside recycling, in which residents are required to place their separated trash out for pickup by trash haulers?

☞ If there is not curbside recycling, are there places that residents can bring their separated trash for recycling? Are these places nearby and open during hours that are convenient for most people?

☞ Does the community provide a place to bring toxic trash such as paints and solvents?

☞ Are businesses in the community required to recycle their trash?

☞ Are there enough trash cans throughout the community to reduce littering?

LOCAL COMPANIES

Some companies are more responsible than others when it comes to how they treat the environment. Some recycle and produce minimal waste, which they dispose of properly. Others are extremely wasteful and carelessly dump poisons into the air and water. Even non-manufacturing companies such as banks and insurance companies can be wasteful if they do not recycle the thousands of pounds of paper they use each year.

Your Green Audit should include the companies in your community. Contact company officials by letter and explain to them that you are surveying local companies for their environmental policies. Ask if you can meet with company officials to ask them a few questions. About a week after you mail the letter, call the company to set up a meeting. Not all companies will be willing to meet with you, of course, but you may be surprised at how many will. (Keep a list of companies that were not willing to meet with you. Make sure to mention them when you release your findings!)

The kinds of things you'll need to find out will differ from company to company. (You can get some ideas by reviewing the school audit earlier.) Here are a few ideas:

☞ Ask a local newspaper what percentage of its newsprint is made of recycled material.

☞ Ask a local fast-food restaurant whether it offers

food packaged in containers that are *not* made of polystyrene foam. Also, ask them whether it encourages its customers to recycle cups, plates, utensils, bags, and other trash.

☛ Ask a local service station whether it recycles used motor oil, and whether they use a device to capture air-conditioning coolant (which contains ozone-destroying chlorofluorocarbons) safely during repairs.

☛ Ask a local grocery store whether it posts signs along the shelves pointing out "green" products.

☛ Ask any company whether it discourages the use of foam coffee cups by making mugs available to employees.

☛ Ask a manufacturing company whether it is in compliance with all federal and local pollution standards.

Your community audit could go on and on. The things you can look into are limited only by your time and energy. Once again, we encourage you to ask as many questions as you can, and to circulate your findings as widely as possible. Keep in mind that in doing your community audit, you are asking questions that probably have never been asked before. That makes you a green pioneer!

Now that you've conducted your Green Audits, turn to the next section for suggestions on what to do next.

Things You Can Do

Now that you understand what's going on—at home, at school, and in your community—it's time to take some action. In this section, we'll offer some simple things you can do to help save the planet, from A to Z.

Keep in mind that it is difficult for most people to do too many new things at once, so it is best to start with only those things you feel comfortable doing. As you do, you will find that many of these things will become easy and natural. For example, once you start thinking about the amount of packaging in the things you buy, it will become an automatic part of your shopping. As you and your family become comfortable with some of the smaller steps, it will be easier to move on to some of the bigger ones.

ADOPT SOMETHING.

An animal, a stream, a whale. There's almost no limit to the number of environmental causes to which you, your friends, or your class can turn. (For more information, contact the Adopt-a-Stream Foundation, P.O. Box 5558, Everett, WA 98201; 206-388-3313; The Whale Center, 3929 Piedmont Ave., Oakland, CA 94611; 415-654-6621; or the American Association of Zoological Parks and Aquariums, Oglebay Park, Wheeling, WV 26003; 304-242-2160.)

AVOID FAST FOOD.

Most fast food is overpackaged and most fast-food companies are responsible for producing mountains of trash. By avoiding fast food whenever possible, you'll help

reduce this needless waste. (For more information about minimizing fast-food trash, contact the Citizen's Clearinghouse for Hazardous Waste, P.O. Box 3541, Arlington, VA 22216; 703-276-7070. For nutritional information about fast food, contact the Center for Science in the Public Interest, 1501 16th St. NW, Washington, DC 20036; 202-332-9110.)

BIKE INSTEAD OF RIDE.

Riding your bike instead of riding in a car saves energy and reduces pollution, of course. But it is also fun! That makes it a double benefit.

BOYCOTT A PRODUCT.

Choose something that you feel is not good for the environment. Once you decide not to buy it, write a letter to the company's president (the address is often right on the package) and tell him or her why you have decided not to buy the product anymore. If lots of people did this, companies would start making more environmentally responsible products! (For more information about starting or joining boycotts, contact the *National Boycott Newsletter*, 6506 28th Ave. NE, Seattle, WA 98115; 206-523-0421.)

BUY PRODUCTS MADE OF RECYCLED MATERIAL.

How can you tell if a package is recycled? Look right on the package. Many have specific claims, such as "made of 100 percent recycled material." However, some recycled packages don't advertise this fact, although there are ways you can find out for yourself. For example, when shopping for cereal, cookies, crackers, and other groceries packaged in cardboard boxes, make sure the boxes are made from recycled paper. It's easy to tell: if the *underside* of the box is gray, the cardboard is made of recycled material. That's good. If the underside is white, it is made of *un*recycled material. That's bad.

CHANGE A LIGHT BULB.

By replacing a standard bulb with a compact fluorescent one (see page 47) you will get more light for less money and save a lot of energy. (For more information on compact fluorescents, contact the Rocky Mountain Institute, 1739 Snowmass Creek Rd., Old Snowmass, CO 81654; 303-927-3128.)

CLEAN UP A STREAM OR PARK.
Get a group of people together—your family or friends or class—and find a stream or park that needs some tender loving care. Arrange for everyone to meet at a specific time to pick up the trash, weed, perhaps even plant some flowers. Ask local businesses to donate money, tools, or other supplies you'll need for the task. You also should invite a newspaper reporter or TV news team to come

along and report on the event. Make sure to check with the proper local authority in charge of the stream or park before starting this project to get permission so you are sure not to break any laws. (For more information, contact the Adopt-a-Stream Foundation, P.O. Box 5558, Everett, WA 98201; 206-388-3313.)

CLOSE THE REFRIGERATOR DOOR.
By leaving it open for just a few extra seconds, you waste a lot of energy. Decide what you want *before* you open the refrigerator door. Then get it and close the door right away.

COLLECT ALUMINUM CANS.
You might raise a lot of money in the process. The best thing is to combine this with your stream or park cleanup (see above). Sell the cans you collect to a local aluminum recycler and use the money for something fun! Or donate the money to a worthy environmental organization (see below).

CONTRIBUTE TO A GOOD CAUSE.
You don't have to contribute a lot of money. In fact, you don't have to contribute any money at all. A local environmental group probably can use your and your friends' help in a variety of ways. By volunteering for just a few hours a week, you'll be making a worthwhile contribution to the environment. It will make you feel really good!

CREATE A COMPOST PILE.

It's easy to do. Find a corner of the yard that's out of the way. Carefully throw food wastes (leftovers, eggshells, coffee grounds, spoiled vegetables, etc.) into a pile and mix with dirt. Every week or so, turn the pile over with a shovel to give it more air. In a few weeks, it will turn into rich, nutritious soil that will help plants grow. Just think: What used to be "garbage" is now a valuable substance!

CUT DOWN ON PACKAGING.

We've already given you several ways to do this. Keep in mind that about half of what we throw away is packaging. By buying products that have as little packaging as possible, you can help to reduce those mountains of trash.

DONATE YOUR TOYS TO A WORTHY CAUSE.

When you get tired of or grow out of your games and toys and other things, don't throw them away. Even if they are broken, they may be fixed and used by other kids less fortunate than you. You'll also be keeping these things out of the trash.

DON'T BUY AEROSOLS.

There are environmentally better packages for most products. Aerosols can't be recycled—which means that they are guaranteed to end up in landfills—and some of their ingredients contribute to air pollution. Instead of aerosols, look for spray bottles, liquids, powders, roll-ons, and other alternatives. (For more information, contact the National Toxics Campaign, 1168 Commonwealth Ave., 3rd Fl., Boston, MA 02134; 617-232-0327.)

DRAW UP A PETITION.

If you find something in your school or in your community you think needs to be changed, one way to convince the people in charge is to circulate a petition, getting as many people to sign it as possible. The petition might say something like: "We, the undersigned, believe that our junior high school should begin recycling all paper, glass, and aluminum immediately, and should place recycling containers throughout the school to make recycling easier." Or, "We, the undersigned, believe that the city government should stop spraying dangerous pesticides in the city park and should find other, less toxic ways of controlling pests." You may want to get a grown-up's help in drafting the petition. Make sure the signed petition reaches the people in charge; send it to the person at the very top. Send a copy of the signed petition to local newspapers and TV stations.

EAT ORGANIC PRODUCE.

Organic produce, as we said earlier, contains far fewer chemicals than other produce. That's probably better for your health, and it is definitely better for the environment. All those chemicals get washed off of farmers' fields into rivers and streams, where they pollute our water. In addition, many of the chemicals are made from petroleum and other nonrenewable resources. So, don't eat chemicals—eat *real* food!

ELECT "GREEN" CANDIDATES.

During election campaigns, ask candidates about their position on the environment. Try to ask specific questions that relate to situations in your community—whether they support a mandatory recycling program, for example, or whether they plan to get tough on polluting companies. You can ask these questions to candidates running for just about any office, because almost every government official makes decisions that affect the environment. The higher up they go, the more people those decisions affect. You might consider a class project in which you ask all of the candidates running for a specific office the same questions. Then compare their answers (or nonanswers) and write an article for a local newspaper about your findings.

FEED THE BIRDS.

Birds need water to drink and food to eat. Feeding birds not only brings a bit of nature to your backyard, it also helps to rid the yard of many kinds of bugs. You can hang a birdfeeder from a tree or place it outside your window, or build a birdbath in your yard from which birds can drink water. There are lots of good books available on birds and birdfeeding. (For more information, contact the International Council for Bird Preservation, 801 Pennsylvania Ave. SE, Washington, DC 20003; 202-547-9009.)

FIND OUT HOW TO DISPOSE OF HAZARDOUS WASTE.

Nearly every household has some kind of hazardous waste: old paint cans, used motor oil, unused pesticides and weed killers. If you dump these things down the drain, you'll end up polluting the water supply. They should be disposed of in a site specially designed for hazardous or toxic wastes. Some cities and counties have monthly or annual pickups. Other areas have special drop-off sites. Call your city or county government to find out the proper way to dispose of such trash in your area. Try organizing a hazardous-waste-collection day in your neighborhood or at your school, encouraging others to dispose of hazardous materials properly. (For more information, contact the Household Hazardous Waste Project, 901 S. National Ave., Box 108, Springfield, MO 65804; 417-836-5777.)

Go to a zoo.

You'd be surprised how much you'll learn about the Earth. Find out how many of the animals in the zoo are at risk of becoming extinct. (Find out how many animals already *are* extinct.) Ask the zookeeper what role humans have played in animal extinction. (For more information, contact the Fund for Animals, 200 W. 57th St., New York, NY 10019; 212-246-2096; or Wildlife Conservation International, New York Zoological Society, Bronx, NY 10460; 212-367-1010.)

GROW A GARDEN.

A garden provides flowers, vegetables, and environmental benefits. It can help reduce soil erosion and may help to reduce some kinds of air pollution. Try to grow your garden using as few pesticides and chemical fertilizers as possible. There are many books and organizations that can help you create an organic or low-impact garden. If your area is suffering from a drought, look into "xeriscaping" (from the Greek word *xeros*, which means "dry"). Your local nursery or agriculture extension may be able to help you or your class to create a garden that can flourish without much water.

Have a "green" picnic.

Plan an outing that doesn't create a lot of waste or pollution. For example, if you're having a barbecue, avoid using lighter fluid—it contains naphthalene, an air pollutant which is suspected of causing cancer. Instead, use an electric starter or, better yet, a device that lets you start coals using newspapers instead of fluid. Use real plates and utensils instead of paper or plastic, and reusable tin or heavy plastic cups instead of disposable paper or plastic ones. Wash the cups

and use them over and over. And set out separate trash bags for paper, glass, and aluminum. Just because you're outdoors doesn't mean you can't recycle.

HOLD ON TO BALLOONS.

Helium balloons—the kind that float up into the sky when you let go of them—are lots of fun, but if you let them fly away, they may harm fish and animals. Helium balloons eventually fall back to earth and can be blown by strong winds miles away into the ocean. Some sea animals mistake the balloons for jellyfish. When an animal tries to eat a balloon, it can kill the animal. So, if you have a helium balloon, hold on tight. If you know of others planning to use them for a celebration, warn them about the dangers of letting the balloons fly away. (For more information, contact the Balloon Alert Project, 12 Pine Fork Dr., Toms River, NJ 08755; 201-341-9506.)

IDENTIFY ENERGY WASTERS.

There probably are several companies in your community that are wasting precious resources. Does a used-car showroom leave its bright lights shining all night long? Do parents waiting to pick up their kids from school leave their cars idling at the curb for a long time? Wherever you see people being wasteful, say something! Write a letter, give a call, or walk right up to them on the street and ask them not to waste our Earth's precious resources.

INSULATE YOUR HOME.

You may find a lot of energy being wasted right in your own home. After you've finished your energy audit, make a list of the things you believe should be done. Your local hardware-store salesperson can help you determine how much the improvements will cost, how much energy they will save, and how much money your family will save in reduced energy bills. (For more information, contact the American Council for an Energy-Efficient Economy, 1001 Connecticut Ave. NW, Ste. 535, Washington, DC 20036; 202-429-8873.)

INTERVIEW SOMEONE IMPORTANT.

There probably are a number of people in your community who make decisions that affect the environment. Politicians, newspaper publishers, corporate leaders, utility executives—all of them make decisions regularly that have an impact on the local, and even national, environment. Interview one of these important people for your school paper, or for a class report. Before you begin your interview, think carefully about what you want to find out. During the interview, make sure your questions are being answered satisfactorily. If not, politely repeat the question, or ask it in a different way.

INVITE A SPEAKER.

A good speaker can provide a lot of useful information and can answer your questions. Almost every environmental group has individuals who will speak to your school or organization, usually for free. Consider hosting a series of speakers, each on a different environmental topic. Even better, invite two people with opposing viewpoints on a single subject—for example, someone from an environmental group and someone from a local factory or public utility. You may be in for an exciting debate!

JOIN AN ENVIRONMENTAL GROUP.

There are hundreds of good organizations around the

country. Most of them have annual membership fees of $25 or less, and some have special rates for kids or students. Try to find one that focuses on something you are particularly interested in. Go to a meeting, event, or other activity. You'll probably meet some other kids with similar interests as yours. (*The Conservation Directory*, which lists information on thousands of national and local environmental groups, is available for $15 from the National Wildlife Federation, 1400 16th St. NW, Washington, DC 20036; 202-797-6800.)

KEEP THE CAR AT HOME.

You've probably learned by now that automobiles are one of the single biggest sources of pollution. Most driving trips are under five miles, and you'd be surprised how many are under one mile. Try walking, biking, skateboarding, rollerskating, or taking the bus.

LEARN ABOUT YOUR COMMUNITY.

We've already described how to do a Green Audit of your community. That's just the beginning. As you travel around your community, watch the local news, or read local papers, keep your Green Audit in mind. Look for things that might be causing environmental problems.

Locate sources of pollution. And make suggestions to people in charge about what you think could be done to improve the situation.

LOOK AT LABELS.

Reading labels can tell you a lot of things. First, you can find out about a product's ingredients—whether it contains anything that might be hazardous to your health or to the environment. A label will also tell you how to contact the product's manufacturer with your questions and comments. Feel free to let them know what's on your mind. Do you think their product is good? Let them know!

Could it be better? Let them know that, too. In particular, let them know if you've decided to buy—or not buy—their product for environmental reasons. Companies listen very carefully to what their customers have to say. It doesn't take very many letters and calls for a company to think seriously about making changes.

Maintain Your Toys.

In fact, keep everything you own in good shape so that it will last as long as possible. By doing so, you are making the best use of the Earth's resources. And when things break, or when you outgrow them, don't automatically throw them away. See if they can be used by someone else. You might think about having a garage or yard sale. (You don't need either a garage or a yard for this—practically any space will do.) You might be surprised how much money you can earn in just a few short hours! Perhaps you'll want to donate some of the money to an environmental organization.

MAKE SCRATCH PADS.

Here's a good way to recycle paper. When you use a piece of paper on only one side, don't throw it away when you are done with it. Instead, put it in a pile with all of the blank sides facing up. When you get a big pile, you can turn the paper into scratch pads. First, get someone to cut the pile of paper in half. (A print shop will probably do this for free or for a few cents.) Then, staple small batches of paper together into "pads." If you really want to do it professionally, purchase a jar of padding compound from a printing supply company or a local print shop. Using a paintbrush, carefully paint a layer of padding compound on one side of the stack of paper. It will dry in a few minutes and you will have made your own scratch pad! (The padding compound will wash off the paintbrush, your hands, and anything else with soap and water.)

NOTIFY THE AUTHORITIES.

Do you know of a polluter? Is a company in your community doing things that are bad for the environment? Don't think twice about reporting them to the local, state, or federal government. You will be doing yourself and your community a big favor. You might even get a reward!

OBSERVE THE THREE Rs.

We described them on page 25: Refuse, Reuse, and Recycle. Whatever you buy, wherever you live, the Three Rs are the most important rules to live by, at least as far as the environment is concerned. The next time you go shopping—whether by yourself or with your parents or friends—think about the Three Rs every time you pull a potential purchase off the shelf. Is it something that is overpackaged or wasteful? If so, Refuse it. Is it something that is made of or packaged in recycled material, or which you can reuse in some way? If so, Re-use it. Is it something that can be recycled easily? If so, Recycle it.

ORGANIZE YOUR FRIENDS.

You've probably heard that "two heads are better than one." Well, ten heads can be even better! You and your friends can probably accomplish a lot if you set your minds to it. Think about the ways you and your friends (or family, classmates, scout troop, or whatever) can help out as a group. Then contact a local environmental group and volunteer your services. Think how much fun everyone can have helping to save the planet!

PLANT A TREE.

We already described all the good things that trees do for us. How would you like to plant your very own tree and watch it grow? There are organizations in most communities that have set up tree-planting campaigns. But you don't even need one of these. Visit a local nursery to find out what kinds of trees will grow best in your area. The nursery people might also help you find a good place to plant a tree (although if you have space in your own yard, that's the best place of all). You can watch the tree's progress every year, and have the pleasure of knowing that you put it there for everyone to enjoy! (For more information, contact TreePeople, 12601 Mulholland Dr., Beverly Hills, CA 90210; 818-753-4600; or Global ReLeaf, P.O. Box 2000, Washington, DC 20013; 202-667-3300; or Trees for Life, 1103 Jefferson, Wichita, KS 67203; 316-263-7294.)

PROTEST ANIMAL CRUELTY

Each year, millions of laboratory animals—rats, mice, dogs, monkeys, and others—suffer needlessly because companies use them to test new products, including most cosmetics and personal-care products. Many of these tests

are extremely cruel. Test animals are routinely burned and injected with poisonous substances, among other tests. The worst part is that many of the products for which they are being used include ingredients that already have been proved safe! Some companies don't conduct these tests. They often label their products "cruelty free" because they do not cause harm to animals. If you had a choice between a product that caused animals to be harmed and a similar one that didn't, which one would you choose? (For more information, contact People for the Ethical Treatment of Animals, P.O. Box 42516, Washington, DC 20015; 301-770-7444.)

Quit Throwing Away Batteries.

Americans go through more than two billion batteries a year to power such things as radios, calculators, watches, flashlights, and computers. Unfortunately, batteries contain many hazardous materials, which leak into landfills when batteries are thrown away. Many of these dangerous chemicals get into our water supply. There are two ways you can avoid throwing away batteries. One is by using batteries that can be recharged over and over. They cost a little more than disposable batteries, but if you use a lot of batteries, they pay for themselves quickly. You should also find out if there are companies in your area that recycle batteries. A growing number of companies are doing so. If you must throw batteries away, do so at a hazardous-waste collection site, if there is one in your area. Still another idea is to send the batteries back to the manufacturers, signifying that you consider used batteries a potential danger. This may encourage companies to begin recycling. In the end, ask yourself whether you really need to use products that require batteries.

Recycle Everything.

Well, not everything, but just about. As we described earlier, there is little you can't recycle one way or another.

One exception is plastic, most of which is not easily recyclable. Set up recycling boxes in your home—one for collecting newspapers, another for collecting other types of paper, another for glass, and another for aluminum. Try

composting (see page 77), which is a way of recycling food and other organic matter. You can even try recycling plastic, if you can find a place that accepts plastic for recycling. If you can't recycle something, see if there is some way you can reuse it.

REUSE A BAG.

You may have gone to the supermarket and heard the checkout clerk ask, "Paper or plastic?" when it came time to put the groceries in a bag. Some people believe that bags made of trees—paper bags—are less harmful to the earth than bags made of chemicals—plastic bags. The fact is, making both types of bags creates a lot of pollution, and both paper and plastic bags use a lot of resources. So neither is much better than the other. The best solution is not to use any bag at all, or to bring your own bag. Some people carry a canvas or mesh bag they can use over and over. If you must use a paper or plastic bag, don't throw it away. Try to use the bag over and over—as many times as you can.

SAVE YOUR CHRISTMAS TREE.

Do you have a Christmas tree every year? What happens to it when the holidays are over? Most people throw their trees away. That's a terrible waste of trees! Instead, have a *permanent* Christmas tree. Designate a tree in your yard as your "official" tree, then trim it every year, right there in the yard. If you don't have a yard , there are many large indoor plants that can serve as your "official" tree. If your family must buy a new tree each year, at least make sure the tree is put to good use when Christmas is over. The boughs can be used in the garden to protect delicate plants during the winter. The needles and cones can be added to a compost pile. The wood can be turned into mulch or wood chips.

SHARE YOUR FINDINGS.

Have you learned something interesting about the environment in your school or community? Have you learned something interesting about a local company or a product being manufactured in your area? Tell the world! By sharing your information, you can help others to pressure polluters, pass new laws, or otherwise make changes that will help the environment. If you are uncertain about whom to tell, ask a grown-up such as your parents or teacher.

SPEND YOUR MONEY WISELY.

When you buy toys and gifts, beware of things made of endangered animals or things made of wood that comes from tropical rainforests. If you're not sure, don't be afraid to ask questions. The more you know about the things you buy, the better decisions you can make. Your spending money is powerful! If you spend it wisely, you can help influence companies to do things that don't harm the environment—or the things that live in it. (For more information, contact Co-op America, 2100 M St. NW, Ste. 403, Washington, DC 20036; 202-872-5307.)

START A WILDLIFE REFUGE.

It's easier than you think! We've already talked about feeding the birds and planting a tree. That's a very good start to creating a place that will attract birds and other animals. By planting the right flowers, you can attract butterflies and hummingbirds. Certain bushes may attract small animals. You can plant wildflowers that will bloom each spring. Just think—wilderness, right in your backyard! (For more information, contact the Backyard Wildlife Habitat Program, National Wildlife Federation, 1412 16th St. NW, Washington, DC 20036; 202-797-6800.)

STOP A LEAK.

If you've done your Green Audit, you've probably already detected the leaks in your home—the leaky water in faucets and toilets, the leaky air around windows and doors—but finding the leaks is only half the battle. Organize a Stop-the-Leak Day on which everyone in your family tightens, insulates, replaces, caulks, and does whatever else is necessary to make your home as "tight" as possible. Your local water, gas, or electric utility company may be able to provide help, or even instructions and supplies. (For more information, contact the American Council for an Energy-Efficient Economy, 1001 Connecticut Ave. NW, Ste. 535, Washington, DC 20036; 202-429-8873.)

STUDY HARD.

It is going to take a lot of very smart people to help clean up the environment in the coming years. If you study hard, you will be able to help future generations solve environ-

mental problems. Learn as much as you can about the way the earth works. Read books, write reports, learn about the science of the planet. As an environmental scientist, you can become a very important person!

SUPPORT GREEN COMPANIES.

In the past, most companies haven't paid much attention to the environment. But now, a growing number are changing the way they do business. Some are changing their products so that they are less wasteful or polluting. Others are encouraging their employees to carpool or to recycle. Still others are helping their local communities improve their environments. These companies deserve all of our support! Whenever you have a choice between supporting one of these green companies or a company that is less green, you should definitely support the greener one. (For more information about corporations' environmental records, contact the Environmental Data Clearinghouse, c/o Council on Economic Priorities, 30 Irving Pl., New York, NY 10003; 212-420-1133.)

TAKE A HIKE.

Or go fishing or bird-watching. Whatever you do, go outdoors to a place where there are as few people, cars, and buildings as possible. Take a look around. Isn't it beautiful? What would happen if all that beauty disappeared because people littered and polluted and harmed the plants and animals? It's important to keep our natural areas in good shape, so that you can enjoy them and your children—and their children's children—can enjoy them, too! So enjoy the great outdoors whenever you can. And if you see some litter there, pick it up and carry it to someplace where it can be safely thrown away or recycled. (For more information on protecting natural areas, contact Defenders of Wildlife, 1244 19th St. NW, Washington, DC 20036; 202-659-9510; Friends of the Earth, 530 7th St. SE, Washington, DC 20003; 202-544-2600;

National Audubon Society, 950 Third Ave., New York, NY 10022; 212-832-3200; or Sierra Club, 730 Polk St., San Francisco, CA 94109; 415-776-2211.)

TALK TO YOUR PARENTS.

There's a good chance that you know more about the environment than your parents do. That's okay, there's still time for them to learn, and you can be the one to teach them. Don't be afraid to share with them the information you've learned in this book and at school. Help them learn about ways they can be Green Consumers and spend their money in ways that will help the environment. Although it doesn't always seem that way, grown-ups *do* listen to kids. If you share your concerns with them, they will become concerned, too. Together, you can help.

TURN OFF THE LIGHTS.

This is such a simple thing to do, but sometimes it's so hard to remember! Ask your parents if you can put little stickers near the light switches you leave on most often, reminding everyone to turn them off when they leave the room. Consider starting a Lights-Off Fund, to which each person must donate a nickel or a dime every time he or she forgets to turn off the lights. As those nickels and dimes add up, you might donate them to an environmental organization.

USE RECYCLED PAPER.

There's just no reason why you shouldn't buy recycled paper whenever it is available. In most cases, it is just as good as "virgin" paper—even better, in fact, because it helps to save trees! You can buy toilet paper, paper towels, napkins, writing paper, books, newspapers, and many other things made of recycled paper. If you or your parents can't find recycled paper products in your local grocery store, ask the manager to stock them.

VISIT A RECYCLING CENTER.

If there's a center nearby, stop and take a look around. Look at all the different things being recycled—lots of different colors of glass, paper, cardboard, cans, maybe even tires and household appliances. Ask the people who run the recycling center what happens to all this stuff after it leaves the center. Think about how wasteful it would be if all that garbage *wasn't* being recycled, but was thrown away instead.

WORK FOR THE ENVIRONMENT.

If you decide to get a summer job, see if there's a job available in which you can help the environment. Most environmental organizations need lots of help, and some

of these jobs can pay you. Check with the local parks department to see if there are any jobs in the parks taking care of plants or flowers. Check with the local zoo to see if you can work with animals. It might be hard work, but it might be a lot of fun. Either way, you can go home each day with the satisfaction of knowing you are helping make the world a better place. (For more information, contact Community Jobs, 1516 P St. NW, Washington, DC 20005; 202-667-0661.)

WRITE A LETTER.

You'd be surprised how much just one letter can do. Most companies don't get many letters from customers, and most politicians rarely hear from the voters, so when they do get letters, they read them very carefully. According to some experts, if a company or politician receives just twenty letters on the same subject within a few weeks, they consider the subject a high priority. You and your classmates can write twenty letters in a few minutes! So, if a company is doing something that you don't like, or if a politican isn't taking actions that can help protect the environment, write a letter. And encourage your parents—and your friends and neighbors—to write letters, too.

E**X**ERCISE YOUR RIGHTS.

As a human being living on the planet Earth, you have the right to clean air and water, a safe environment, and the unspoiled beauties the world has to offer. You should speak firmly and loudly against those people and companies who threaten to take those rights away from you by polluting or by making decisions that encourage polluting or other wasteful behavior. That's the only way that you can be sure that the world will still be just as beautiful when you are an adult. If you don't dream of a better world—and do something about it—no one will do it for you.

Y ELL AT A LITTERER.

Well, maybe you don't have to yell, but if you do see someone littering, you definitely should say something. Be polite, but state your case. Explain that littering not only is ugly and costs us money (because we have to pay people to pick up the litter and dispose of it), it is also bad for the environment.

Z ERO IN ON SPECIFICS.

While we've covered a wide range of environmental problems and solutions in this book, you can be most effective by choosing one or two specific problems to focus on. Don't try to do everything at once. Pick a problem—acid rain, for example, or animal cruelty—and learn as much about it as you can. Find the individuals and organizations in your area working on the problem and see how you can get involved. That will make you a powerful Green Consumer!

Where to Learn More

Have you gotten a little "greener"? We hope so. But don't rush. Going green can take time. Don't expect to be able to do everything right all at once. You'll only get frustrated and discouraged. The key is to do what you can do—what is comfortable and natural. The more things you do, the easier things get. Eventually, you'll wonder why everyone isn't as green as you!

In this final section, we've listed some things you might want to read, and some organizations you might want to contact. Many of these organizations have special publications and programs just for kids.

THINGS YOU CAN READ

Here are some books we think are worth checking out. Not all of them are still in print, but most of them can be found at a local library—perhaps even the one in your own school.

Bodies of Water; Fun, Facts, and Activities, by Caroline Arnold (Franklin Watts, 387 Park Ave. S., New York, NY 10016; 212-686-7070, 800-843-3749. 1985; not in print)

Chadwick the Crab, by Priscilla Cummings (Tidewater Publishers, Box 456, Centreville, MD 21617; 301-758-1075. 1986; $5.95)

The Kids Nature Book: 365 Indoor/Outdoor Activities, by Susan Milord (Williamson Publishing, Church Hill Rd., Charlotte, VT 05445; 802-425-2102, 800-356-8791. 1989; $12.95)

Endangered Animals, by National Wildlife Federation (Ranger Rick Books, 1400 16th St. NW, Washington, DC 20036; 202-797-6800. 1989; $19.95)

Fifty Simple Things Kids Can Do to Save The Earth, by The Earth Works Group (Andrews & McMeel, 4900 Main St., Kansas City, MO 64112; 800-826-4216. 1990; $7.95)

It's Your Environment: Things to Think About, Things to Do, by the Environmental Action Coalition (Charles Scribners Sons, Front and Brown Sts., Riverside, NJ 08075; 800-257-8247. 1971; not in print)

Keepers of the Earth, by Michael J. Caduto and Joseph Bruchac. (Fulcrum, Inc., 350 Indiana St., Ste. 510, Golden, CO 80401; 303-277-1623, 800-992-2908. 1989; $19.95)

The Lorax, by Dr. Seuss (Random House, 201 E. 50th St., New York, NY 10022; 212-751-2600. 1971; $10.95)

Nature for the Very Young, by Marcia Bowden (John Wiley and Sons, 605 Third Ave., New York, NY 10158; 212-850-6276. 1989; $10.95)

The Ocean Book, by The Center for Environmental Education (John Wiley and Sons, 605 Third Ave., New York, NY 10158; 212-850-6276. 1989; $11.95)

P3: The Earth-Based Magazine for Kids (P3 Foundation, P.O. Box 52, Montgomery, VT 05470; 802-326-4669. $14 for 10 issues)

Planet Earth series: *The Oceans, Coastlines, Water on the Land, The Work of the Wind*, and *Weather and Climate*, by various authors (The Bookwright Press, 387 Park Ave., New York, NY 10016; 212-686-7070, 800-843-3749. 1988; not in print)

The Planet of Trash: An Environmental Fable, by George Poppel (National Press Inc., 7201 Wisconsin Ave., Ste. 720, Bethesda, MD 20814; 301-657-1616. 1987; $9.95)

Poisoned Land: The Problem of Hazardous Waste, by Irene Kiefer (Atheneum, Macmillan Publishing Co., 866 Third Ave., New York, NY 10022; 800-257-8247. 1981; $12.95)

Professor Noah's Spaceship, by Brian Wildsmith (Oxford University Press, 200 Madison Ave., New York, NY 10016; 212-679-7300. 1987; $4.95)

Project Ecology book series: *Air Ecology, Animal Ecology, Plant Ecology, Urban Ecology*, and *Water Ecology*, by Jennifer Cochrane. (The Bookwright Press, 387 Park Ave.

S., New York NY 10016; 212-686-7070, 800-843-3749. 1988; not in print)

Save the Earth! An Ecology Handbook for Kids, by Betty Miles (Macmillan Publishing Co., 866 Third Ave., New York, NY 10022; 212-702-2000. 1988; not in print)

Sierra Club Summer Book, by Linda Allison (Sierra Club Books, 730 Polk St., San Francisco, CA 94109; 415-776-2211. 1989; $7.95)

Sierra Club Wayfinding Book, by Vicki McVey (Sierra Club Books, 730 Polk St., San Francisco, CA 94109; 415-776-2211. 1990; $13.95)

Weather Watch, by Valery Wyatt (Addison Wesley Publishing Company, Inc., Jacob Way, Reading, MA 01867; 617-944-3700. 1990; $8.95)

The Wump World, by Bill Peet (Houghton Mifflin Co., 1 Beacon St., Boston, MA 02108; 617-725-5000. 1974; $3.95)

ORGANIZATIONS YOU CAN CONTACT

Many of these organizations offer special publications and membership to kids. Below are some of our favorites.

Alliance to Save Energy (1725 K St. NW, Ste. 914, Washington, DC 20006; 202-857-0666) offers a free poster "Pulling Energy Out of a Hat." Also available free is *Your Home Energy Portfolio*, a guide designed to help recognize energy conservation opportunities in your home.

Center for Marine Conservation (1725 DeSales St. NW, Ste. 500, Washington, DC 20036; 202-429-5609) offers an ocean activity book (K–6) for $8.95. The center also has an Adopt-a-Beach program.

The Children's Rainforest (P.O. Box 936, Lewiston, ME 04240; no phone) has free information about how you can organize and raise money to purchase and protect an acre of rainforest. Send a self-addressed, stamped envelope.

Coastal Conservation Association (Amy Richard, P.O. Box 1630, Fulton, TX 78358; 512-729-7426) has a magazine, *Rising Tide*, for kids, for a $10 membership fee. The magazine teaches about underwater ecosystems and lets you know how to get involved in your area.

Cousteau Society (930 W. 21st St., Norfolk, VA 23517; 804-627-1144) offers *The Dolphin Log*. It discusses humans' impact on the sea. A subscription is free with a family membership ($28), or $10 a year by itself.

Creating Our Future (398 N. Ferndale, Mill Valley, CA 94941; 415-381-6744) offers manuals ($5) on how to become an activist and how to get involved in environmental and rainforest issues.

Defenders of Wildlife (1244 19th St. NW, Washington, DC 20036; 202-659-9510) has a free magazine, *The Comeback Trail,* for students (50¢ per copy in bulk). It covers current wildlife conservation issues and teaches basic ecological concepts.

Earth Communications Office (P.O. Box 36M39, #207, Los Angeles, CA 90036; 213-932-7968) offers a free booklet called *Cry Out: An Illustrated Guide to What You Can Do To Save the Environment.*

Hug the Earth (P.O. Box 621, Wayne, PA 19087; 215-688-0566) helps kids understand the environment and sponsors monthly workshops and other activities. Family membership, including a monthly newsletter, is $15 a year; classroom memberships are $1 per student.

Izaak Walton League of America (1401 W. Blvd., Level B, Arlington, VA 22209; 703-528-1818) offers an S.O.S. (Save our Streams) kit for $5 that includes a newsletter, *Splash*, a stream survey, a stream insect identification guide, an erosion fact sheet, and project ideas.

Kids Against Pollution (P.O. Box 775 High St., Closter, NJ 07624; 201-784-0668) has memberships for $15 a year that include a newsletter and information packets. It provides a forum through which to trade success stories.

National Wildlife Federation (1400 16th St. NW, Washington, DC 20036; 202-797-6800) offers a free "Backyard Habitat" kit that teaches how to build a nest box for birds and how to encourage animals to habit your yard. There is also a Nature Education Catalog that offers videos, publications, games, and discovery kits, as well as lots of information.

Nature Conservancy (1815 N. Lynn St., Arlington, VA 22209; 703-841-5300) has a free information packet for kids, including a fact sheet on the importance of maintaining species' diversity.

Sierra Club (730 Polk St., San Francisco, CA 94109; 415-776-2211) offers a kids' packet for 25¢ that lists environmental organizations with kids' programs.

Take Pride in America (P.O. Box 1339-Y, Jessup, MD 20794; 800-446-4253) has free posters, buttons, decals, and a Youth Guide, which details participation in a national program to conserve America's natural and cultural resources.

Trees for Life (1103 Jefferson, Wichita, KS 67203; 316-263-7294) offers a $2 tree-planting packet, part of Project Trees for Life, including seeds, instructions, information, a container, and a poster. There are also buttons ("Trees for Life," "Kids for Trees") for $1 each, which support Trees for Life projects in other countries.

U.S. Department of Agriculture (U.S. Forest Service, P.O. Box 96090, Washington, DC 20250; 202-447-4543 has a free booklet, "How a Tree Grows," and a poster, "Why Leaves Change Color."

U.S. Department of Energy (Conservation and Renewable Energy Inquiry Referral Service, P.O. Box 8900, Silver Spring, MD 20907; 800-523-2929) has a brochure, "Learning About Energy Conservation" (FS218), which offers helpful tips with pictures to color.

U.S. Environmental Protection Agency (Office of Communications and Public Affairs, 401 M St. SW, PM211B, Washington, DC 20460; 202-382-2080) will send free information booklets on acid rain, air and water pollution, recycling, and other topics, as well as a coloring book. *Earth Trek* is a free booklet that explains pollution to kids.

Whale Center (3933 Piedmont Ave, Ste., #2, Oakland, CA 94611; 415-654-6621) has an "Adopt a gray whale calf" program for kids. For $25, you will get a photo of a whale calf, an adoption certificate, quarterly updates, and activity sheets.

World Wildlife Fund (1250 24th St. NW, Washington, DC 20037; 202-293-4800) will send a free elephant poster including information about elephants and the ivory trade, and a list of what you can do to help.

Vegetarian Resource Group (P.O. Box 1463, Baltimore, MD 21203; 301-366-8343) has a free coloring book, "I Love Animals and Broccoli," promoting a healthy breakfast. Send a self-addressed, stamped envelope.

WRITE TO US!

We want to know what you think. What did you find easiest about "going green"? What was hardest? Let us know! Did you conduct a Green Audit? If so, send us a copy! Do you have any green tips you'd like to share with other kids? Send them to us. We'd be happy to hear anything you'd like to tell us about your experiences in going green. Write to us at:

The Green Consumer
1526 Connecticut Ave. NW
Washington, DC 20036

INDEX

106

ACKNOWLEDGMENTS

A number of people on both sides of the Atlantic Ocean contributed to this effort, and they deserve recognition and thanks:

Steve Bonnist, Intermediate Technology Development Group; David Cameron, Books for a Change; Karen E. Firehock, Izaak Walton League; Michael Gaffney, Wordscape; Jackie Gear, National Centre for Organic Gardening; Isabelle Gore, SustainAbility; Libby Grundy, Council for Environmental Education; Stephanie Hutter and Beth Jordan, Viking Penguin; Treva Mathur, Trees For Life; and Cathryn Poff and Elizabeth Pollock, Tilden Press.

About the Authors

John Elkington and **Julia Hailes** are co-founders of Sustain-Ability, "the green growth company," which aims to promote environmentally sustainable economic growth. They are co-authors, with Joel Makower, of *The Green Consumer*. Mr. Elkington and Ms. Hailes live in England.

Joel Makower is a Washington, D.C.-based writer on consumer and environmental issues and the editor of *The Green Consumer Letter*, a monthly newsletter. He has written or co-written more than a dozen books.

Tony Ross is a well-known British children's book illustrator, whose works include *Earthlets* and *Fantastic Mr. Fox* by Roald Dahl.